Transformation, Miracles, and Mischief

Transformation, Miracles, and Mischief

The Mountain Priest Plays of Kyōgen

Translations with Commentary

Carolyn Anne Morley

East Asia Program
Cornell University
Ithaca, New York 14853

The *Cornell East Asia Series* publishes manuscripts on a wide variety of scholarly topics pertaining to East Asia. Manuscripts are published on the basis of camera-ready copy provided by the volume author or editor.

Inquiries should be addressed to Editorial Board, East Asia Series, East Asia Program, Cornell University, 140 Uris Hall, Ithaca, New York 14853.

for my parents

TABLE OF CONTENTS

Acknowledgements

I have been most fortunate in my teachers. Donald Keene guided me through my dissertation out of which this book emerged. I cannot thank him enough for his advice and encouragement. He will always be the ideal of the literary scholar after which I strive. I am endlessly indebted to Nomura Mansaku, my kyōgen teacher and friend, for accepting me as his pupil and for opening his acting life to me. If anything here rings true it is due to Nomura Mansaku who exudes the warmth, good humor, and affection of kyōgen in every aspect of his life. Koyama Hiroshi first introduced me to the study of kyōgen texts at Tokyo University and has since carefully corrected my sometimes misguided ideas. He has opened many doors in the closed world of traditional theater. I am deeply grateful to him. Kobayashi Seki has spent many hours discussing kyōgen with me as well as sharing his extensive library. He has been both a friend and a teacher. Monica Bethe has been an inspiration both through her life and her scholarship. Karen Brazell read the initial draft and gave me many important suggestions which I have tried to incorporate. My friend Marilyn Sides read through preliminary drafts. Her evident enjoyment of kyōgen as well as her insightful comments have been instrumental to the completion of this book. A special thanks is owed to Robert Lobis, as he well knows. I also would like to take this opportunity to express my gratitude to the Japan Foundation for a summer grant and a five-month fellowship which made my research possible. There are so many others to thank: Shannon Nakaya, Hyde Hsu, Lisa Cohen, and Winnie Olsen for their work in seeing the final draft to completion, and many more besides. Finally, where would I be without my husband Hiroaki Kuromiya's unswerving faith in this book? In fact, I can even say that it is at his insistence that this book appears at all.

List of Photographs and Illustrations

(All of the photographs contained in this volume are by courtesy of Yoshikoshi Tatsuo)

A Mountain Priest (Nomura Mansaku in *The Snail)*

FOREWORD

Kyōgen are one-act, comic skits which date back to the fourteenth century in Japan. Traditionally, they are performed as interludes between the serious dramas of noh. The subjects of the plays are mundane: quarrels between husbands and wives, farmers' disputes, mischievous servants, ignorant masters, self-important priests, drinking parties, household gods, and even miracles that occur on one's own hearth. Kyōgen plays are based on speech and mime rather than on music, dance, and poetry as we would find in noh. While humor is their outstanding characteristic, they offer as well a pleasing simplicity, both in conception and in performance. For example, the highlight of the play *Kuriyaki* (Chestnut roasting) is a solitary scene in which a servant sits cross-legged by the kitchen fire roasting chestnuts. The setting, the mime, and the accompanying monologue all draw us into a strangely familiar scene of hearth and home. The sense of intimacy generated by kyōgen is felt by non-Japanese audiences as well. Recent performances by Nomura Mansaku in the United States of the play *The Snail* excited members of the audience into chanting the chorus of nonsense lines as they left the theater. Actual audience participation is not a feature of kyōgen but the reaction of the American audience is indicative of the involvement they felt with the actors on stage.

This kind of sudden intimacy is what attracts Japanese viewers as well. At one time a common cultural context could have been presumed for kyōgen audiences; today that very intimacy is produced by the actors through techniques which have evolved over the years to fill the growing gap between the stage and the audience. The art of the kyōgen actor lies in creating a character-type on stage and then repeatedly dismantling it to reveal the man within the myth, a process referred to by Nomura Mansaku as "slipping in and out of the character." This is made possible, paradoxically, by the stylized and choreographic patterns of kyōgen performance; nothing in kyōgen is improvised. Slight alterations in tempo or vocalization produce the illusion of spontaneity. The characters seem easily accessible to the contemporary audience, at the same time as they provide a window into medieval commoner society. The past surfaces in the present through the living actor, and a public performance merges with a more intimate private gathering.

My purpose in this study is to analyze the kyōgen acting technique

3

with regard to the main character-type, and to show how this style of acting developed over time in response to audience expectation. When we look at kyōgen performance today, we must keep in mind that for the first two hundred years of its history, from the fifteenth through the sixteenth centuries, it was an improvisational form. The authors of the plays, some two hundred and sixty of which form the current repertory, are with few exceptions anonymous. That is to say, the plays and the character-types which appear in them changed in response to the audience with each performance until they were finally recorded in the seventeenth century. The intimacy that was later accomplished by artistry was the original basis for kyōgen humor. In fact, that there are blanks where names might be expected in some of the plays suggests that names of people in the audience may very well have been substituted into the play on the spot. The greater complexity of the noh plays which involve music and dance has meant that the texts and their authorship have been preserved in many cases. Kyōgen, on the other hand, is an actors' theatre. There are no directors, no producers, and no authors of the plays.

A Drunk Tarō Kaja rests on his master's lap (Nomura Manzō in a *Lying Down Song*).

My interest in the unique atmosphere of the kyōgen stage was sparked by the first kyōgen play I attended. I present my experiences here as illustrative examples of the unusual intimacy between audience and actors characteristic of kyōgen performance. The play which I saw was *Neongyoku* (A Lying Down Song). The scene remains vividly before me. The late Nomura Manzō, in the role of Tarō Kaja (the servant), sat cross-legged in the middle of the stage, stubbornly refusing to sing for his master without a drink. His long-suffering and increasingly impatient master finally gave in and dipped his open fan, pouring, "dobu, dobu, dobu," into Tarō Kaja's waiting cup. Manzō leaned forward and sniffed the air. "Drink, drink," he was urged, and Manzō lifted his fan carefully in his hands, gulped, and gazing out into the audience, smacked his lips, "Ahh. . . delicious!" The large bare stage seemed to shrink to an intimate circle around the two as Manzō's face began to flush, his eyes to droop, and a slight scent of sake seemed to waft over the audience. The sake-drinking scene later became a familiar one to me but the feeling of direct contact with the actor through the main character is a fresh surprise with each performance.

Much later, I came upon a short essay entitled "The Moon and the Kyōgen Actors" (1949) by the twentieth century novelist Tanizaki Jun'ichiro in which a similar atmosphere of almost casual intimacy is described. The essay is about an informal moon-viewing party consisting of actors of the Shigeyama family and their friends on the grounds of Nanzen temple in Kyoto. The homeliness of the scene–the spontaneous bursts of kyōgen song and dance–is peculiarly evocative of actual kyōgen performances. Moreover, the light-hearted interjection of kyōgen song into the party must have been closer to what kyōgen performance was like originally, during its long years of improvisational performance at parties and festivals. Tanizaki describes the effortless manner in which the group joins in when the elder Shigeyama Sensaku begins to sing a kyōgen ditty:

> Without ceremony, the venerable Sensaku began quietly
> to intone under his breath,
>> "Zaazaa, they rustle, zaazaa they rustle,
>> the Yoshino pines where the lovely maid passes.
>> She comes to serve sake but she is carrying her child.
>> With a child in her arms?
>> Never, it won't do!
>> With a child in her arms?
>> Oh never, it won't do!
>> From the lord and master, she hides the child away,

> but just as they begin to doze,
> through the window the moon shines brightly.
> Oh hurry! Hang it out, a long cotton belt!
> Hang it from the eaves, a narrow sleeve!
> Tonight's moon, this moonlit night,
> shines brilliantly, all around. . ."
>
> Mr. Yamanouchi's mother joined in, followed by all who
> knew the words, their voices growing louder and louder
> until they reached a crescendo with "through the window,
> the moon shines brightly. . ." [1]

The party of actors seems to invite us to join in, much as I felt myself to be a co-conspirator in Manzō's drinking party on stage. In other words, the border between stage and audience seems peculiarly blurred in kyōgen, as if, like Tanizaki, we were guests at the home of a friend.

Sensaku's comments on the essay in his memoirs, *Eighty Years of Kyōgen*, are equally revealing. In a public but highly personal response, Sensaku writes, "I was taken by surprise when "The Moon and the Kyōgen Actors" appeared in a magazine. My name, my son's, and my grandson's names all appeared along with details about our moon-viewing at the home of Ueda Ryūnosuke in the Nanzen temple grounds. From time to time my name does appear in newspapers and such but this was the first time that the name Sensaku appeared in such a fine essay. I had my grandson read it to me over and over again, feeling somehow tickled and pleased." [2] There is an assumption here that the writer and his readers are all members of the same group, an assumption reminiscent of exchanges characteristic of popular literary circles in an earlier period. This expectation underlies the esthetics of kyōgen as well. When watching kyōgen, we experience an illusion of intimacy with the actors on stage. In the same way, however removed we are in actuality from the inner circle of the Shigeyama family, we are seduced into believing ourselves privy to their innermost thoughts.

The secret of kyōgen humor lies in the unique relationship which evolves on stage between the actor, his role, and the audience. For this reason, I have chosen to make the lead character-type the focus of this study: the character is the vehicle of communication between the stage and the audience. The actor who performs the lead character has the *shite* role. The secondary role is known as the *ado* role and any subsequent roles are labeled *koado*. Most plays consist of two or three roles. The shite actor is the only one who, seemingly, slips out of character. He controls the audience response to his character and to the play. The significance of the main character was recognized by kyōgen actors from at least the seventeenth century, as we can see from the early grouping of the plays according to the shite role by the Ōkura school. The categories of characters are representative of their generic nature: gods (*waki kyōgen*); warlords (*daimyō*); bridegrooms/mountain priests (*muko/yamabushi*); demons/small landlords (*oni/shomyō*); women (*onna*); priests/blindmen (*shukke/zatō*). There is also a category for miscellaneous plays. Other methods of organization exist but most actors today designate plays according to character-type. The plots often seem to be pieced together from two or more individual plays, a reflection of kyōgen's long improvisational tradition, and do not lend themselves to systematic organization.[3] Once the texts were set down in writing, actors began to redirect their efforts to interpretation and acting technique. The categorization of the plays by the shite role occurred simultaneously with the first recording of the plays in full.

If we consider the texts alone, kyōgen comedy seems most akin to the plays of the commedia dell'arte or to medieval European farce. The plays are short comic skits in one act, fifteen to forty-five minutes in length, and appear as interludes during a program of noh. Almost no props are used and costumes reflect actual clothing of the period. The repetitive plots, the use of stock characters drawn from commoner society of the medieval period, and such simple comic devices as role reversal, repetition of an action or phrase, trickery, and mistaken identity would seem to identify kyōgen with the broad and energetic humor of the farce. However, Western comedy evolved from farce into the satires of Molière and the English comedy of manners, while the changes in kyōgen took place within the genre itself. The only parallel would seem to be with the eighteenth century Italian comedies of Goldoni which grew directly out of the commedia dell'arte tradition. In Goldoni, however, we have an identifiable author, and the authority of the text soon superceded the authority of the earlier acting tradition. Other forms of drama, such as *kabuki*, developed in Japan too but they did not displace kyōgen. Kyōgen continued to evolve in terms of the refinement of the acting method until it developed into the highly choreographed comic performance of today.

The lead character-type (the shite role) is created on stage by means of a series of performance patterns. We can define kyōgen performance patterns as recognizable sequences of speech and mime which recur from one play to the next. The internal rhythm for the performance patterns is known as *jo-ha-kyū* and consists of a gradual increase in tempo and complexity. In noh, this same tempo is observed throughout the play from individual sections to the process of the play as a whole. Kyōgen follows the jo-ha-kyū rhythm only within set performance patterns. When an actor breaks the rhythm, and this is only partially evident in the written text, he is able to project his stage persona to the audience. In this way the actor infuses the character with his own personality and is able to bridge the gap in time from kyōgen's origins in the fifteenth century to the present.

In spite of the importance of the shite role to the projection of spontaneity and intimacy on stage, interest in defining performance patterns necessary to the creation of the main character-type has been relatively recent. In fact, even in the case of noh, the now widely accepted analysis of the written text by performance patterns or segments (shōdan) is a modern phenomenon initiated by Yokomichi Mario.[4] The first analysis in English of noh as performance was done by Bethe and Brazell in *Nō as Performance: An Analysis of the Kuse Scene of Yamamba*. No similar analytical study of kyōgen has been undertaken largely because of the eclectic nature of the kyōgen plays. Nevertheless, certain patterns, long recognized by the actors, are now codified in the written texts. They are of little interest to us except when viewed in relation to the creation of the shite role, at which point they become critical to our understanding of the kyōgen acting technique.

The patterns noted down in recent editions of kyōgen plays include the *nanori* (self-introduction), the *michiyuki* (travel pattern), and the closure pattern; each has a self-contained sequence of speech and mime. Variations in content occur depending on the character-type. For example, the master in a master-servant play tends to introduce himself in the same way with the same intonation from one play to the next: "I am a neighbor" ("Kore wa kono atari ni sumai itasu mono de gozaru").[5] The *daimyō* (lord) on the other hand usually announces, "I am a daimyō known throughout the eastern provinces" ("Tōgoku ni kakuremonai daimyō desu").[6] In addition to the generic performance patterns, particular character-types may have additional patterns unique to them. In some cases, the character patterns are difficult to discern while in others, such as the mountain priest, they are rich and provocative due in large part to kyōgen's close association with noh. In fact, we are forced in the case of the mountain priest to expand our limited definition of a pattern to include those sequences defined by a metrical formality adapted from noh, specifically, the *shidai* (introductory chant) and the incantations. The result is a loose definition of a pattern but one that is more suited to kyōgen, which in any case does not translate into a number of identifiable modules of music, speech, and dance as does noh.

The eight plays translated here are all from the mountain priest category of plays. The mountain priest is an important figure for kyōgen. Mountain priests were known to perform their own versions of noh and kyōgen plays at the end of their long ritual retreats in the mountains. They were, therefore, both the subjects and the actors of the plays. Moreover, like the kyōgen actors in their assumption of roles, the mountain priests were deeply involved in the world of transformations and magic. Since the majority of the original audience for kyōgen, as well as the actors and the characters who appear in the plays, were commoners, a study of the mountain priest plays affords us a glimpse into the common man's understanding of the concept of miracles and the role they played in his life. We see in these plays both an underlying belief in the possibility of miracles and an ironic look at unquestioning or ignorant believers.

Chapter one introduces the kyōgen genre and the mountain priest plays in particular. What was the commoner's understanding of miracles and transformations and of the mountain priest's role in them? In order to understand the signs of the mountain priest character, we must first appreciate some of the underlying assumptions of medieval man, at least insofar as we can determine them from the plays and from popular tales of the period. A healthy skepticism existed along side belief in the miraculous from the first, but there is an edge to the mischief in the early versions of the plays owing to the belief in the possibility of miracles. The focus of the humor shifts in later texts to accommodate a more sophisticated city audience, but the manifest desire to believe in magic remains. Those who are so foolish as to believe indiscriminately become the butt of kyōgen humor. In this respect the mountain priest fares no better than any other character. When his powers fail, he is ridiculed; on the other hand, they do not necessarily fail. The shift in favor of skepticism in the later texts is a shift of emphasis only, and is responsible for the ironic tone which predominates in kyōgen today.

In chapter two, the acting method is viewed in a historical context in order to examine how changes in the audience and the times affected the development of the actor. Kyōgen is neither didactic nor does it display the wish-fulfillment theme of many of the popular tales (*otogizōshi*) of the same period. Instead we find in kyōgen clear evidence of the secularization of theater which allowed the comic actor to comment unreservedly on the foibles and weaknesses of the average man.

Chapter three presents a close reading of the play, *The Crab,* in order to explain how the text changed to accommodate the changing climate of the times. It includes texts from the three kyōgen schools and from the three most prominent developmental periods for kyōgen. For the later period, I have emphasized the Izumi and Ōkura schools because the third school, the Sagi, died out except in remote areas by the early nineteenth century. I have also referred to the *Kyōgenki,* a text in three volumes from the seventeenth and eighteenth centuries unrelated to any of the formal kyōgen schools.[7]   Koyama Hiroshi speculates that the first volume (1660) provided the text for the amateur group of performers known as the Nanto negi ryū, located in Nara. It was the first text of kyōgen to be published. The second volume (1700) and the third (1730) reflect, to varying degrees, the influence of the Ōkura school on the amateur troupes. For pre-Edo sources I have relied on the only text available, an early collection of plot summaries known as the *Tenshō bon* (1570).[8] The early Edo texts I have used are the *Ōkura Toraaki bon* (1642)[9] and the *Izumi Tenri bon* (the *Kyōgen rikugi* text) (1646).[10] For the mid-eighteenth and the nineteenth centuries, I have referred to the *Ōkura Torahiro bon* (1792),[11] the *Izumi Kumogata bon* (1818-1830)[12] and the *Sagi Kenjirō Kentsū bon* (1855).[13] The Ōkura school *Yamamoto Tōjirō bon*[14] of late Edo and the Izumi school *Sanbyaku banshū*[15] and the *Kyōgen shūsei*,[16] also of late Edo, are standard texts for current performance.

As the selection of texts indicates, kyōgen underwent two distinct developmental phases. During the first two or three hundred years, from the fourteenth to the sixteenth centuries, kyōgen was an improvisational theater. Aside from the *Tenshō bon*, the only information we have about kyōgen comes from tangential references to performances in diaries of the period. In the early seventeenth century the plays were recorded for the first time and three professional schools of actors formed: the Ōkura, Izumi, and Sagi schools. The texts from this early period are transitional in nature and are followed in the eighteenth and nineteenth centuries by a formalization of the texts.

Chapter four concludes the discussion of the plays with an analysis of the kyōgen acting method as seen in the performance of the mountain priest character. Specifically, I have asked the following questions: what are the performance patterns and where do they originate, and, how does the actor manipulate audience expectation of the character in order to create the character-type? I have been influenced in my approach by Keir Elam's work on the Czech school of theater studies, *The Semiotics of Theater and Drama*, [17] which is a collection of essays concerned with the concept of a performance text. Accordingly, the written text is viewed as one element, along with various dramatic elements including gesture, vocalization, and costume, involved in the creation of the character-type on stage. I have also been greatly influenced by the works of Monica Bethe and Karen Brazell who discuss performance texts for noh and incorporate the written text into their discussion. For kyōgen, I have had to develop a slightly different approach in order to allow for the vital role of the kyōgen actor's own stage persona in the creation of a comic character. I have done this by analyzing the performance patterns which emerge in relationship to the character in the play *Persimmons* and the breaks that occur in the performance patterns. By inserting these breaks in tempo, voice production, or gesture, the actor is able to project his own personality and communicate directly with the audience. A sense of spontaneity, essential to humor, is thereby generated on stage. These breaks are not apparent from the written text alone. I have approached the character from a variety of perspectives: the history behind the patterns associated with the character-type in the performance text; assumptions the audience makes about the character based on the historical figure of the mountain priest, as well as on its appearance in tale literature and noh plays; and the systematic interruption of expected patterns of performance as a means of freeing the actor's personality to issue forth. The final chapter concludes the discussion of the centrality of the character-type to kyōgen humor.

Part I: Commentary

I
TRANSFORMATIONS

Theater in any age is about transformations, but in medieval Japan,[1] where social transformations could occur almost overnight, the concept of transformation took root in the popular imagination, affecting nearly every aspect of life, whether physical, spiritual, or social. In fact, there is a disturbing lack of distinction made in this period between miraculous physical changes and those changes in status brought about by upheavals in society. For the commoner, sudden movement up or down the social scale was as incomprehensible as the depictions in picture scrolls of the period showing people in various stages of transformation: priests turned into snakes, for example, or jealous women into serpents. Confusion about the nature of transformation is, as we shall see, a rich source of irony in kyōgen, especially as the plays evolved in later periods.

In part, the fascination with transformation lies in the Buddhist world-view as it was understood by the general populace. William LaFleur claims that we can gain an insight into the popular understanding of Buddhism through the ninth-century collection of stories by Kyōkai in *Nihon koku genpō zen'aku ryōiki* or *Nihon ryōiki* which the author presents as proof of the workings of the Buddhist law of karmic causality.[2] Kyōkai preaches the Buddhist truth that one's actions in this life result in rebirth in one of the six modes of being (*rokudō*) in the next life. Often the incidents related are of unusual physical transformations taking place within an individual's lifetime, such as a woman turning into a cow from the waist down.[3] These too are explained as evidence of karmic change. While the great Buddhist texts were impenetrable for the average man, the stories of miraculous changes in *Nihon ryōiki* worked their way into popular belief through their adoption by priests promulgating the Buddhist doctrine. In their efforts to proselytize among the illiterate, priests and nuns as well as their lay counterparts would travel the country with picture scrolls with which they could entertain as they taught simple truths. They could be found seated by the roadside, a collection of bells and other instruments to produce sound effects at their sides, awaiting the approach of a passerby. By the fourteenth and fifteenth centuries, their peregrinations would have brought them into contact with the kyōgen actors, some of whom also numbered among the vagabond entertainers of the period.

We should not be surprised then to find the kyōgen actors playing with the idea of transformation in all of its permutations. While a naive and indiscriminate belief in transformation is generally ridiculed in kyōgen, the possibility of transformation as one of the fundamental principles of life is not. In fact, without such a belief, the poignancy of the humor would be lost. An understanding of this seeming contradiction – the upholding and simultaneous ridiculing of a belief – is essential for the appreciation of the mountain priest plays in which transformations and miracles have a significant role. In the course of a single play the mountain priest's powers may be both acknowledged and denied. For example, in *Persimmons* a mountain priest first fails to transform himself into a falcon, then succeeds in trapping his tormentor with a spell, and finally is duped by the self-same tormentor. Or, in *Owls,* the mountain priest's spell does summon forth the owl spirit, but in the end the priest himself is possessed by the owl. Kyōgen does not deny the existence of the supernatural powers of the priest. Rather, the man who cannot measure up to the myth of the powerful ascetic is revealed in all his human frailty.[4] As William LaFleur has pointed out, in kyōgen the clever and streetwise inevitably come out on top. A robust, self-mocking humor informs even the earliest versions of the plays regardless of the character portrayed. This kind of ironic and unblinking look at the common man is what entitles kyōgen to be called "realistic" theater despite the stylization of the acting method.[5]

A Mountain Priest successfully prays a fleeing man to a halt (*Persimmons*).

Before examining the mountain priest plays in more detail, we need to have a clearer sense of how transformation and miracles were popularly understood. In kyōgen, the characters often use the concept of transformation actively, in order to argue themselves out of difficulties, or as a means of deceiving someone. In *Hito wo uma* (Man into horse), for example, a man tries to hire himself out as a servant by announcing that he can change men into horses. When the master commands him to change the servant, Tarō Kaja, into a horse, the man takes Tarō Kaja aside and explains that he's never done this before so they'll just have to pretend. At first the master is pleased, but when the horse continues to look like Tarō Kaja, the master scolds both the man and the servant and chases them off. On the other hand, there are also plays in which transformations and miracles are treated quite seriously. In *Tsurigitsune* (Fox trapping) a fox transforms himself into the priest Hakuzōsu in order to approach a hunter and convince him not to trap foxes. The verb used for transformation here is "*bakete iru*" which can mean anything from "disguised" to "transformed." Taking into account the many tales about fox spirits tricking men, we can probably assume that an actual transformation is intended. Certainly, this is how it appears on stage. In any case, the humor does not lie in the transformation but rather in the gullibility of the man who cannot see through the fox's ruse, and, later, in the weakness of the fox who cannot resist the meat set out in a trap. The fox, still in his priestly disguise, seems eerily half man and half fox as he sniffs longingly at the trap.

Although Satake Akihiro states categorically that in the mountain priest plays the priest's powers necessarily go awry, this is not always the case.[6] In one of the mountain priest plays at least the miraculous powers of the mountain priest are treated quite seriously. *Tsuto Yamabushi* (The lunchbox thief) features a mountain priest who successfully pits his spells and incantations against the thief who stole a woodcutter's lunch. Significantly, in this instance the thief, rather than the mountain priest, is the object of humor which may account for its deviation from the usual theme: the ineffectuality of the mountain priest's powers. In fact, in early versions of the play the thief is cast as the main character, removing the play from the mountain priest category altogether.

The popular understanding of transformation becomes clearer when we examine the play *Nari agari* (Upward bound). Through folk aphorisms and specious reasoning the character's imagination leaps from natural, physical changes to social and miraculous transformations. The term *nari agari* was in popular usage in the medieval period and referred to sudden promotions in social status.[7] In the play, Tarō Kaja attempts, through a series of non sequiturs, to lead his master to accept that his missing sword has turned into a bamboo stick. What is interesting here is Tarō Kaja's own willingness to believe in his theory. Tarō Kaja has been put in charge of his master's sword during a night vigil at Kiyomizu temple. Both master and servant doze off, giving a shyster the opportunity to snatch the sword, leaving his bamboo stick in exchange. "Oh no!" Tarō Kaja exclaims upon awakening, "I was supposed to be guarding my master's sword but it's turned into [nari agari] a bamboo stick!"[8] As they travel home, Tarō Kaja continually steals glances at the stick, hoping to see it change back into a sword but to no avail. When his master asks if he heard any interesting stories at the temple, Tarō Kaja offers him a number of examples of transformations, intending to lead up to the sword. His master listens at first without interest. Tarō Kaja begins, "They say in this world, a bride quickly becomes a mother-in-law." And then, "They say puppies soon grow up to be dogs; they say bitter persimmons ripen and become sweet." Finally, he introduces a miraculous story of sorts. "They say it's quite true that mountain potatoes turn into eels." The master acknowledges that he's heard this before but that he is not convinced. Tarō Kaja insists, " No, no! They say it's a fact. You see, it can rain continuously in the fourth and fifth months which causes landslides in the mountains. Mountain potatoes tumble out during the slides and fall to the bottom of the valley and there they turn into eels, so they say." The master's ears perk up at this, and he asks if Tarō Kaja has heard any other such stories. "Well," says Tarō Kaja, "the district supervisor is a very rich man and he has a famous sword. To anyone else it looks like a snake and if someone should shout "thief!" it leaps right out of his hand and chases the thief away. Now, isn't that a miracle?" The master is impressed, and Tarō Kaja is encouraged to continue. "You know, they say that usually when a man is rising in the world [nari agari], all the objects around him rise with him. So, it looks like there's some good luck coming to you, too." Picking up the stick, Tarō Kaja announces that the master's sword has transformed itself into a stick and, since any change is an omen of fortune, it follows that the master must be about to rise in the world. The master realizes what has happened and scolds Tarō Kaja for his carelessness and stupidity. The easy shift from the plausible to the fanciful and from natural phenomena to social change is probably a fairly accurate representation of thinking in the period, at least as we are led to believe from pre-kyōgen collections like *Nihon ryōiki* and from later collections of tales as well.[9] The humor of the *Nari agari* play lies both in the fact that a sword is said to "have moved up" [nari agari] to become a stick instead of the reverse, which we would expect, and in Tarō Kaja's desire to believe his own story. In other words, the concept is valid but Tarō Kaja's use of it is not.

Examples of this kind of facile belief in the miraculous are recorded in *Kanmongyoki* (Diary of Prince Sadafusa of Fushimi). According to one account, in the seventh month of 1416 a Jizō Buddha fell to earth at Horikawa. People brought gifts to mark the event. Three months later it came to light that this seeming miracle was a trick contrived by some wicked priests.[10] This incident appears to be the model for the kyōgen play *Niō* in which a gambler, down on his luck, dresses up as a Niō statue (the giant statue of one of the fierce guardians of the Buddha, two of which are generally placed at the entrance to a temple). A friend broadcasts the news of the Niō's descent to earth, and pilgrims come to leave alms. The gambler is so successful in his ruse that, despite his friend's urging, he cannot bring himself to quit. Finally, a lame man comes and rubs his leg on the Niō's foot which is extended in the air. The ticklish gambler, unable to restrain himself, bursts into laughter. He is chased off by the angry pilgrims. The gambler, like the wicked priests in the *Kanmongyoki* account, creates the pretense of a Buddhist statue in order to trick the simple and naive. The very size of the Niō, however, makes the kyōgen story immediately humorous. Although he loses all the alms he had collected, the gambler exits laughing. Apparently, the trick, alone, was worth his trouble.

The harmless delight that the gambler takes in his impersonation is a constant theme in kyōgen and lends the plays a childlike charm. In the play *The Snail* a boy mistakes a mountain priest for a snail, and the mountain priest is so amused by the thought that he quickly supplies proof of his identity with his black cap, his shell (either a conch shell used by the mountain priest as a horn, or the mountain priest's sleeve), and his horns (his mantle). He then leads the boy down the road chanting to a strong hypnotic beat a children's song about a snail.

> Since it neither rains nor blows,
> if you don't come out, I'll crush your shell.
> If you don't come out, I'll crush your shell!
> Come out, come out, snail, snail;
> come out, come out, snail, snail!

The boy's father appears and challenges the priest, but soon he too becomes mesmerized by the song. There is no purpose to this false transformation. The mountain priest is simply enjoying his mischief. He is as successful chanting a ditty as he is in other plays with an actual incantation.

Sometimes, an unwitting transformation fools both parties concerned. In one of the early mountain priest plays found only in the *Tenshō bon* text (1570), *Oni matsukaze* (The Demon and the Matsukaze Chant), a servant on his way home with costumes he has borrowed for a festival of noh performance meets a mountain priest. The two take shelter from a sudden shower and the mountain priest dozes off. The servant, worried about the costumes, takes out a demon mask to dry it. He puts it on and begins, incongruously, to chant from the noh play *Matsukaze*. The noise wakes up the mountain priest who finds himself confronting a demon. He is so alarmed that he runs off. Meanwhile, the servant too becomes alarmed by the priest's reaction and, assuming there must be an actual demon in the room, rushes off after the priest. The servant is blind to his own transformation, which in any case is an illusion.

In a similar vein, in the play *Nukegara* (Shedding the Demon Shell) an unreliable servant, Tarō Kaja, falls into a drunken stupor by the side of the road instead of completing the errand on which he has been sent. He is discovered by his master who decides to play a trick on him by tying a demon mask to his face. Tarō Kaja awakens with a heavy feeling in his head and wanders off to get some water from a nearby pond. When he looks down, he sees a demon reflected in the water and leaps backward in alarm. He does not want to be thought a sissy so he steels himself for another glance. A second look convinces him that not only has he seen a demon but that he himself is the demon. The actor, as Tarō Kaja, stands on tiptoe and wriggles his hands exaggeratedly in the air, dancing back and forth, as he watches his reflection in the water. He weeps when he realizes that at some time during his drunken stupor he has been transformed into a demon. The incongruousness of the angry grimace of the demon mask and Tarō Kaja's sadly slumping shoulders and pitiful weeping brings to mind the famous routine of the French mime Marcel Marceau. Marceau mimes putting on the two masks that symbolize the stage, the comic and the tragic masks (although, in fact, Marceau uses his own facial expressions and no mask at all). Suddenly, he finds that he cannot remove the laughing mask. His body is contorted in misery as he pulls and twists his face in his efforts to remove the gaily smiling mask. In the kyōgen play we have a more human and realistic conclusion. Tarō Kaja makes his way home, forlornly, and appeals to his master to take him in. After all, he cries, who will befriend him now that he has become a demon? But the master refuses to have a demon around to frighten his guests, and he turns Tarō Kaja away. In his misery, Tarō Kaja throws himself on the ground, determined to take his own life. The jolt knocks off the mask. Tarō Kaja's reaction is a combination of embarrassment and tremendous relief; the nightmare is over. Mask in hand, he returns to his master and announces that he has shed his demon skin and is ready to come back to work. The master scolds him and chases him off stage. Tarō Kaja's embarrassment is a clear indication that he has understood the master's trick but he pretends innocence, hoping to get into his master's good graces by becoming a conscious partner in the ruse.

In each of the examples given above there is a willingness to believe in the miraculous that leaves the characters open to trickery and self-deceit. If we look back to the *Niō* play, for example, the belief that a Buddhist statue in some form or another might fall to earth is not in itself the source of the humor. After all, the incident recorded in *Kanmongyoki* of the Jizō falling to earth is not considered humorous. The humor of the kyōgen play lies in the absurdity of believing that an object of the immense size of a Niō statue could be thought to fall to earth. In other words, kyōgen is not denying the possibility of miracles but rather exposing the human side of misplaced belief. This is exactly what we see in the mountain priest plays as well.

The interest in transformation fades somewhat during the Edo period, and there is a corresponding change of focus in the plays. This is due in large part to a change in the audience who were now predominantly city dwellers and, among them, government bureaucrats who were more sophisticated and less interested in legends than earlier audiences. Perhaps equally important, however, was the establishment of the highly structured Tokugawa regime which all but eliminated the earlier phenomenon of upward mobility [nari agari]. In addition, officially sponsored Confucian learning began to displace the earlier fascination with the Buddhist doctrine of karmic change among the populace at large. This is not to suggest that an interest in magic and transformation disappeared altogether or that it was eliminated from the plays. Rather, we see a shift in the focus of the humor. The persistence of legends integral to the plot in plays like *Niō* indicates a conscious decision on the part of the actors to retain some of the flavor of an earlier period. There were many reasons for choosing to do this. For example, by setting a play in an earlier period the kyōgen actors could avoid offending the elite in the audience with their sometimes barbed humor.

In most instances, however, the actors responded to the changing interests of the audience by dropping arcane elements from the plays. *Persimmons*, for example, was originally a play about transformation, but in the later texts the humor shifts to mimicry instead. In the *Tenshō bon* text (1570), the play appears as *Kakikui yamabushi* (The Persimmon-Eating Mountain Priest). A mountain priest comes upon an orchard of persimmon trees, climbs a tree, and sets about satisfying his hunger. The orchard's owners (there are two in *Tenshō bon*) appear and, catching the mountain priest up in the tree, decide to play a trick on him. They announce that they've discovered a falcon in their tree and that if it's a falcon, it will fly. The mountain priest waves his arms about, attempting to fly, but falls to the ground. In this early version the humor is rooted in the myth of the mountain priest's ability to transform himself into a falcon. In later texts in the early Edo period, the humor shifts and a whole array of animals is added to the falcon. Once the belief in transformation lost its timeliness, the humor of the play changed direction, and the actors concentrated on mimicry. Other plays less versatile than *Persimmons*, *Man into Horse*, for example, were dropped from the repertories or are simply no longer performed.[11] The survival of the plays depended on a change of emphasis in order to appeal to vastly different audiences in different periods.

A mountain priest pretending to be a monkey (*Persimmons*).

The emergence of kyōgen as an identifiable and independent comic form is the subject of the following chapter. Since the history of kyōgen is first and foremost the story of the evolution of the comic actor, I have tried to follow the actor through time. This has not been an easy course to pursue due to the paucity of written records available. Unlike the noh actor we find the comic actor on the very margins of society until at least the seventeenth century. As a result the kyōgen actor has been open to influence from every direction, and the kyōgen genre has been enriched and renewed at each juncture along the way to becoming a discrete comic form.

The position of the actor outside of mainstream society is not unique to kyōgen. Noh actors too were no more than itinerant performers until the early fifteenth century, and indeed the same may be said for early performers in most areas of the world. However, in the case of kyōgen the situation continued for centuries longer than was true for noh. Victor Turner defines such marginal members of society as those functioning in a liminal mode, that is to say, on the threshhold of normal life. He sees their role as that of allowing society to express the forbidden without destroying itself and, in so doing, reaffirming its values.[12] Accordingly, entertainers, vagabonds, village fools, and others living outside of mainstream society were free to express the repressed wishes and desires of that society, virtually turning the society upside down. The reversals of roles and mockery of beliefs in kyōgen can easily be interpreted in this vein. In other words, the actors felt free to mock the naive and the ignorant regardless of social status precisely because basic beliefs and social values were in no way endangered thereby.

Turner's explanation offers a legitimate alternative to the social science-oriented analysis of early postwar Japanese scholars such as Hayashiya Tatsusaburo and Matsumoto Shinpachiro, who saw such role reversals as realistic representations of turmoil in society at the time.[13] The society of medieval Japan has been characterized as upside down (*gekokujō*), in that peasants could become landowners overnight, and landowners might lose all of their status and wealth. There are, however, too many inconsistencies within the kyōgen genre to support this view; in kyōgen, the master is not inevitably on the losing end and the poor and afflicted are ridiculed at least as often as the successful and wealthy.[14] In any case, if we take as our basic premise that kyōgen is intended to be comic, any interpretation that ignores the humor of the plays seems doubtful at best. To understand what was felt to be humorous in different periods we must look closely at the changes in the attitudes of the actors and in their audiences.

II.
TRACKING THE ELUSIVE COMIC ACTOR

We do not know much about the comic actor before the seventeenth century. Both the noh and kyōgen theaters evolved out of earlier dramatic forms known as *sarugaku* [1] and *dengaku*,[2] and we see occasional mention of early comic performance associated with these genres. In *Shin sarugakki*, the diary of Fujiwara Akihira (988-1066), there is a record of *sarugaku* offered at the Inari festival at Horikawa palace in Higashi shichijō in Kyoto.[3] In addition to such entertainments as puppetry, juggling, and tightrope walking, there are several comic skits: the sage priest Fukukō seeks a priestly vestment; the nun Myōkō goes begging for diapers; and a country gentleman visits the capital. The theme of the first skit seems very close to the kyōgen play *Fusenaikyō* (Sermon without a donation) in which a priest pretends to have forgotten his vestment at a patron's home in order to have an excuse to return to collect his alms. The "country gentleman in the capital" theme is one that recurs frequently in the kyōgen repertory. The skits seem to indicate an early interest in satire which is foreshadowed by satire and parody in the official court performances of the eighth century. In *Kyōkunshō*,[4] a record of official court music, there is a passage describing the consecration ceremony of the Great Buddha at Tōdaiji (782) in which there are several *gigaku* plays (masked mime) parodying important religious personnages.[5] We know, too, that among the *bugaku* (court dance) pieces there was one entitled *Ama* which was accompanied by a parody, *Ninomai*.[6] The Ninomai dancers, wearing the masks of a leprous old man and woman, enter the stage toward the end of the formal dance and, as the dancers exit, proceed to parody their movements.

While the comic pieces cited above were integral parts of a formal performance, comedy was often performed informally and by nonprofessionals. One such informal performance is mentioned in the *Uji Shūi Monogatari* (A Collection of Tales from Uji). Two minor musicians who happen to be brothers are participating in a ritual *kagura* (shrine music and dance) when they are asked by Emperor Horikawa (1079-1107) to perform a *sarugaku*. They conferred over what to do and one brother suggests:

> I'm going to get into the bright light of one of
> the bonfires, pull my skirts right up and show

my bony legs. Then I'll call out, "It's v-v-very
l-l-late, I'm f-f-frozen stiff, I th-th-think I'll w-
w-warm m-m-my b-b-balls," and run around the
fire three times.[7]

His crafty brother dissuades him and then goes on to perform it himself.
The emperor and all present explode in laughter. Significantly, the term
sarugaku is used here to refer specifically to impromptu comedy and is performed by two musicians rather than by professional comic actors. The
comic actor of this period was still a marginal figure who improvised on
the spot like his Italian counterpart in the sixteenth century the *comici*
(later known as the commedia dell'arte). In their total irreverence the early
"actors" seem to participate in the carnivalesque humor identified by
Bakhtin in his thesis on medieval Western popular humor.[8] Although
tempered by the requirements of audience and period, this strain continues
in kyōgen's easy embrase of apparent contradictions in values and beliefs.

The salty humor cited in *A Collection of Tales from Uji* seems to
have been enjoyed by early audiences. However, we also have evidence
that satire, in particular, could prove offensive. An entry in the
Kanmongyoki (Diary of Prince Sadafusa of Fushimi) tells us that on the
eleventh day of the third month in 1424 a sarugaku troupe was invited to
perform at Prince Sadafusa's private residence in Fushimi. They
performed a "kyōgen" satirizing the impoverished nobility and were
roundly reprimanded. Prince Sadafusa took the performance as a personal
affront directed at his own financial difficulties.[9] In another entry the same
actors were chased off Mount Hiei where they had been performing before
the monastery. Apparently, they had dressed up as monkeys, the sacred
messengers of Mount Hiei, and had offended the monks. As Prince
Sadafusa tells us, the problem was one of impropriety.[10]

Early postwar Japanese scholars have used these incidents as evidence that kyōgen plays depict the actual situation in the society of the
time, a society turned upside down by constant warfare and upheaval.
However, the comic license appropriated by the actors was offensive only
insofar as no esthetic distance had been established between the audience
and the stage either by dramatic convention or by custom. By the time this
had been accomplished in the seventeenth century, plays reversing the roles
of lords and vassals, masters and servants, husbands and wives and so on,
were readily accepted by an audience composed, in part at least, of government dignitaries.

The next substantial reference to kyōgen is found in *Shūdōsho*
(1430), a critical commentary by the first major figure in the noh world,

Zeami Motokiyo (1363-1443). His alarm at the license taken by comic actors performing with noh is evident in the following admonishment:

> Kyōgen itself would merely be considered vulgar if its only aim were to make the audience laugh boisterously on all occasions. It is said that true gaiety lies within a delicate smile and such impressions are always effective and moving for an audience. . . . Whether in terms of words or gestures, a kyogen actor must, avoiding all vulgarity, allow his well-born audience to experience humor that is both clever and endearing. To repeat again, just because a performer's function requires him to be amusing, there should certainly be no need for him to use vulgar words or gestures. This matter should be considered carefully.[11]

Zeami's concerns about the kyōgen actor led him to formulate the first dramatic conventions for the kyōgen actor within a noh play. He writes, under the heading "The functions of the kyōgen actor":

> It is well known that their method of creating amusement for the audience in the form of comic interludes involves the use either of some impromptu materials chosen at the moment or of some interesting incidents taken from old stories. On the other hand, when these actors take parts in an actual noh play, their function does not involve any need to amuse the audience. Rather, they are to explain the circumstances and the plot of the play that the audience is in the process of witnessing.[12]

In other words, a kyōgen role was now established within noh and we can assume that some kyōgen actors were loosely attached to the four *sarugaku* guilds. Zeami describes the two functions of the kyōgen actor as they are defined today: as an actor in comic interludes (*honkyōgen*), and as an actor within a noh play (*aikyōgen*). As Zeami specifies, the aikyōgen was to explain the events of the play in the vernacular.[13] This was necessary as noh plays were written in literary Japanese which was difficult to understand even when first composed. Today, the kyōgen passages, using colloquial language of the fifteenth and sixteenth centuries, are almost as difficult to understand as the noh. Since the text for the aikyōgen was the property of the kyōgen actors, the noh actors had trouble controlling the kyōgen parts. *Shūdōsho* contains warnings to both the kyōgen actors and the waki (secondary role in noh) actors not to deviate from the script.[14]

Zeami's attempts to define the kyōgen role and kyōgen humor suggest that he may have had more than a little trouble with the comic actors. The inclusion of a comic role at all in the noh repertory must have been in response to audience demand. Before Zeami's day, flute or vigorous dance pieces (*rambyōshi*) had been used as interludes, but by Zeami's time the kyōgen skit was used exclusively.[15]

Comic actors (*okashi hōshi*) are occasionally mentioned by name in performance records, although this is unusual in that the kyōgen pieces, because of the high degree of improvisation, were rarely counted as official parts of the program. The earliest mention of comic actors appears in a record of the Ceremony at Kasuga Wakamiya Shrine in 1349.[16] In addition to *sarugaku* performed by vestal virgins of the shrine and acolytes, two comic actors are listed as performing comic dances: Harutada and his partner Hisaharu. The pieces do not seem to have been comic skits such as we later come to expect of kyōgen and add to the ambiguity of the early comic actor's role. Later, in the record of the subscription performance at Tadasugawara in 1464, there is mention of the kyōgen actor Usagi. This same Usagi appears in a collection of criticisms, *Yozayakusha mokuroku*, by the Kanze school drummer Jigayozaemon Kunihiro (1506-1580), confirming the authenticity of the Tadasugawara record.[17] Usagi's son was later claimed by the Sagi school as one of its ancestors.

While some of the identifiable kyōgen performers were attached to guilds and performed on a regular basis with noh, many more must have performed sporadically at local shrine festivities or wandered the country as itinerant entertainers, stopping off at castle towns or by the roadside to offer impromptu skits. Zeami attacks one such rustic performer called Yoshihito Ue, as follows:

> Among kyōgen performers, there was an actor
> named Yoshihito. (Although he was well
> known in the country) he was never brought to
> the capital because of the shallowness of his art.
> Those in the capital who knew little of the
> nature of his performances said, "perhaps it is

because Tsuchidayū was afraid of being overwhelmed by him." In fact, however, Yoshihito ue was not at all talented, in spite of his far-reaching yet empty fame. Indeed he was scoffed at by those from his own province. If one has a real grasp of the differences between performances in the country and in the capital, then the significance of this matter will be clear.[18]

The Tsuchidayū to whom Yoshihito ue is compared seems to be the younger Tsuchidayū, son of an actor whom Zeami praises earlier for the grace (*yūgen*) of his comedy. Zeami's predilection for a sedate form of humor casts some suspicion on his statement that Yoshihito ue was "not at all talented." Perhaps his performance was closer to that mentioned above in the Uji collection than Zeami would have wished. In *Sarugaku dangi*, Zeami is said to have told the following anecdote concerning the younger Tsuchidayū :

Once when Tsuchidayū the second was near the shogun's northern villa (in the suburbs of Kyoto) he passed by a high government official at Takahashi. Realizing that the passerby was Tsuchi, the official hid his face behind his fan and walked on. Tsuchi came close to the official in order to sneak a look at him, then put up his fan as well to hide his own face and walked on. This kind of attitude reveals the soul of a truly gifted player.[19]

Zeami reserved his admiration for this kind of understated mimicry and looked down on more blatant forms of humor.

Unfortunately, very little is known of the early kyōgen plays prior to the plot summaries collected in *Tenshō bon* (1570). Of the list of twenty titles of kyōgen which appears in the 1464 record of the subscription performance at Tadasugawara, a number bear titles similar to those in the current repertory, but there is no way of ascertaining the content of the plays. Kyōgen was still at an improvisational stage of development, and the variations in the performances of a single play must have been great.

Toward the end of the sixteenth century kyōgen appears to have grown in popularity. Amateur groups proliferated around the capital of Kyoto and in the free port city of Sakai, as well as in the newly emerging castle towns. The most striking evidence of this new popularity is the 1593 performance by the three great generals of the day, Toyotomi Hideyoshi, Tokugawa Ieyasu, and Maeda Toshiie. They proceeded to tweak noses and pull ears in a rendition of the play *Mimihiki* (known today as *Igui*).[20] The boy Igui, tired of being perpetually tapped on the head with his master's fan, obtains a magic hat which renders him invisible and allows him to tweak his master's nose. As the performance by the generals suggests, the appeal of kyōgen reached across class boundaries to every sector of society.

During the sixteenth century, the names of kyōgen actors begin to appear more frequently in historical records. The *Yozayakusha mokuroku* (Jigayozaemon Kunihiro, 1506-1580) mentions two actors from the generation preceding the author's own, Genzaemon of the Kanze noh school, and Yazaemon of the Komparu noh school. Both are linked to Mangorō,[21] an actor whose name appears only in this context but who is subsequently claimed by all three schools of kyōgen as their ancestor.[22] Yazaemon is said by Kunihiro to be the father of his contemporary, Ōkura Yazaemon Toramasa. From here the lineage for the Ōkura school, at least, is well documented thanks to Toramasa's grandson, Toraaki, author of a book of criticism, *Waranbegusa,* as well as the *Toraaki bon* collection of plays. Toraaki tells us that Toramasa was bequeathed the name "Tora" by Lord Nobunaga and that it was used by the family from that time on. Toramasa's son, Torakiyo, is said to have received the enthusiastic patronage of Toyotomi Hideyoshi.[23]

There seems to have been no conciousness of "school" among kyōgen actors in this transitional period. Toramasa, his son Torakiyo, and even his grandson Toraaki performed on the same stage with a variety of different actors including self-styled amateurs and members of the Chōmei family (later called the Sagi school). For example, the father-and-son team of Ōkura Toramasa and Torakiyo performed at a subscription performance in 1592 at Shichidōgahama in Sakai (recorded in Meireki sakai shichidō kyōgen shibai, 1655) along with Chōmei Jirō and the well-known amateur actors of the Nanto negi group, Toppa and Sosuke.[24] Such all-kyōgen performances gave the actors the opportunity to expand and develop their repertory. In succeeding years, after Hideyoshi designated the four Yamato sarugaku noh guilds for patronage, the all-kyō-gen programs ceased. Individual kyōgen actors began actively to seek affiliation with the noh troupes; the renowned Chōmei Jirō, mentioned above, quickly joined the Kongō school[25] and Toraaki, for one, stopped performing with amateurs or with professionals of other families in order to perform exclusively with noh.

Several currents converged to induce actors to form schools, record texts, and formalize their performances. One of these was the increasing popularity of kabuki. The seductive dances of the female prostitutes doubling as dancers which gave rise to kabuki proved a particularly powerful allure for the city audiences. As early as the late sixteenth century, kyōgen actors (all male) were taking comic roles (*saruwaka*) in the kabuki. The ease with which the kyōgen actor slid into kabuki was quite predictable considering the highly improvisational nature of both arts at the time. The link between kabuki and prostitution resulted in outbreaks of violence among the spectators who vied for the attentions of the performers. In 1629 women were banned from kabuki, and by 1652 the troupes of young boys (*wakashū*) which had formed to fill the gap were banned as well for the same reason. A year later, in 1653, the Tokugawa government gave permission for kabuki performances by adult males (*yarō kabuki*), provided they consisted of full-length plays rather than erotic dances or scenes of seduction.[26] Interestingly, these plays were known as *monomane kyōgen zukushi.* The term "kyōgen" had come to designate any dramatic skit based on real life situations and using dialogue rather than song and dance. Eventually, to avoid confusion, kyōgen came to be known as *noh kyōgen.*[27]

The threat of the imminent dissolution of kyōgen into kabuki stimulated actors to preserve their own art form. The move toward consolidation of the plays was at once a reactionary and a radical one: reactionary because it meant retaining comic forms from an earlier era, but radical because it demanded that the actors attempt for the first time to articulate and formalize their art, a process which in and of itself transformed kyōgen into classical stage comedy.

The possibility of kyōgen's absorption by kabuki, like the disappearance of the comedia dell'arte into the plays of Molière and Shakespeare, only hastened a trend already under way. Another motivation behind the actors' decision to produce written texts and establish schools was the promise of patronage by the new Tokugawa government. The decisive battle of Sekigahara in 1600 had brought to a close years of warfare. With the inauguration of the Tokugawa shogunate Japan was to enjoy more than two hundred years of relative peace and stability under centralized, bureaucratic rule. The Tokugawa rulers sought to systematize their policies based on their understanding of neo-Confucian philosophy borrowed from China. Accordingly they were drawn to establish an official state theater in keeping with the Confucian dictum regarding the importance of music to good rule. The Tokugawas, not surprisingly, chose noh, and with it, kyōgen. In this they displayed the innate conservatism that was the hallmark of their government. At this point, the influence of noh becomes more apparent in the development of kyōgen. Whereas in the decades immediately preceeding the Tokugawa era, kyōgen surpassed noh in popularity, from this point on the kyōgen actors performed almost exclusively with noh, on a noh stage, and before an audience which had assembled for the purpose of viewing noh.

In their effort to be recognized by the noh schools and thus to receive official patronage the kyōgen actors began to form schools. A formal document indicating authorship of a number of plays, submitted to the government in 1721 by Ōkura Yatarō Torazumi, can be seen as one attempt of the Ōkura school to legitimize its lineage. Although the document is largely a fabrication, it attests to the concern of the actors for authentic family lines.[28] Family in this instance refers to the household unit (*ie*) which was one of the basic building blocks of Tokugawa society. The members of a household were not necessarily blood relatives, although each had a direct relationship of some kind to the head of the family. For the kyōgen actors to be regarded seriously, they had to organize themselves into this basic household unit. Even before the Tokugawa (Edo) period the Ōkura family was a recognizable presence in the theater world, so it is not surprising that it was the first family to formally establish itself as a school of kyōgen.

During Toraaki's lifetime, the Ōkura school's eminence was challenged by the Sagi school. The surge into the limelight of the Sagi actors was due, in part, to their connection with the Kanze noh troupe, popular with the shogunate in the seventeenth century, but also to their affinity with the kabuki theater. Toraaki's cranky remarks concerning the Sagi actors in *Waranbegusa* were not devoid of professional jealousy. He describes the Sagi as upstarts who obtained their repertory by copying the Ōkura school. The earliest Sagi text, *Yasunori bon*, appeared about a century after the *Toraaki bon* text, so Toraaki's complaints may have had some legitimacy. The name Sagi (heron), he notes disdainfully, was adopted by the school because Sagi Niemon's father lived near a swamp in Isoshima and had an incredibly long neck.[29] Toraaki goes on to complain bitterly:

> The kyōgen popular today is tasteless. The dialogue is unintelligible: garbled and confused. The lower classes may laugh at facial contortions, mouths hanging open, and pop-eyed expressions, but any person of culture would be offended by such vulgar antics. They are no different from the fool (doke) so popular in

kabuki.[30]

Professional jealousy aside, Toraaki was pointing out one of the clear differences between his school and the more flamboyant Sagi school. The general tenor of his remarks is echoed in the theatrical criticism of the day, *Kindai yozayakusha mokuroku* (Kanze Kenzaemon Motonobu, ed., 1646). Toraaki must have been particularly piqued at the preference of the Tokugawas for such rough and vulgar humor over the more refined humor of his own school. In fact he tells us, in *Waranbegusa,* that the Ōkura school is criticized for being too close in style to noh.

There are instances recorded in *Kindai yozayakusha mokuroku* which convey the displeasure of the government with at least some of the antics of the Sagi school. When Sagi Niemon leaped off the stage on a hobby horse and rode through an audience composed of the shogun's party, he was punished with a month-long jail sentence.[31] In another instance, Toraaki quotes Tajima Yagyū, a noted martial arts master, who reported an incident in which an entire performance of New Year's ritual noh, *Okina sanbasō,* had to be repeated because the Sagi actor in the role of Senzai [32] mimicked a puppet.[33] These are clear breaks in the formally established esthetic distance. In one case, the actor violated audience space; in the other he ignored the accepted form for his role.

While the Ōkura and Sagi schools were vying for the patronage of the shogunate in Edo, the Izumi school established itself in Kyoto, performing for the court as well as receiving the patronage of the Owari branch of the Tokugawa family. The earliest text of the Izumi school, *Kyōgen rikugi* (hereafter referred to as *Tenri bon)* is closer in format to the earliest collection of plays, *Tenshō bon,* being a collection of plot summaries with only songs and poems recorded in full. The Izumi school was slower to establish itself than the Ōkura and Sagi schools. In the end, the first head of the Izumi family Mori Motonori did not have the necessary influence to create a school on his own and was forced to join up with two active amateur groups, led by Miyake Tōkurō and Nomura Matasaburō. Together they became known as the Izumi school.[34]

Probably because of the longer period of interaction with amateur groups, the Izumi texts retain a more distinctive flavor of commoner life than do the Ōkura texts. If we compare the Izumi *Tenri bon* and the Ōkura *Toraaki bon,* we find that long sequences of dialogue used to describe a scene or an emotion are entirely missing from *Toraaki bon* which instead favors light-hearted repartee. *Toraaki bon* emphasizes dramatic elements while *Tenri bon* includes intimate scenes with psychological appeal but with little relevance to the plot. The difference in audiences is perhaps crucial here. The Ōkura school, located in Edo, placed its main emphasis on appealing to the samurai elite, while the Izumi school continued to perform in Kyoto in less formal settings, often with amateur actors, and appealed to a mixed audience, the majority of whom were city dwellers of commoner status.

If we look, for example, at the *Tenri bon* version of the play *Moraimuko* (Receiving a Son-in-Law), in which a couple's quarrel leads the wife to demand a divorce, we find various domestic details included. When the couple part, the husband hands his wife a *kosode* robe as the required proof of the divorce. The *kosode* was common wear during this period for both men and women and therefore a natural choice. The husband of the *Toraaki bon* version, however, hands his wife a sword. Clearly a sword would have been of greater interest to the samurai audience in Edo. In a subsequent scene, the wife returns to her father and complains of her husband's abuse. In *Tenri bon* the father attempts to reason with his daughter and to point out his sake-loving son-in-law's good points.[35] We can imagine such a scene of domestic discord even today. However, the scene diverges from the mechanism of the plot and is cut from *Toraaki bon*. *Toraaki bon* has a crispness lacking in *Tenri bon* but achieves this at a cost of depth.

As kyōgen became more and more a theater for the initiated rather than a popular form such as kabuki, the effect of its close association with noh became more pronounced. A gradual refinement of the acting method began to take place. Toraaki complained of the vulgarity of the kyōgen of other schools but, in fact, when we compare his texts with those of a later period, they are still strikingly crude. For example, in the play *Neongyoku* (A Lying Down Song), the drunk Tarō Kaja claims to have mistaken his master for his wife and purses his lips as if to kiss him on the cheek. None of the later texts include this scene. Or, among the "woman" plays, many close with either the man carrying the woman or the woman carrying the man piggyback off stage. The compilers of the later texts rigorously eliminated almost all body contact. A rather startling example of a crude attempt at realism is found in *Chūkichi*, in which the actor is told to apply a red camelia blossom to his nose to simulate having had his nose shaved off.[36] Such theatrical gestures were really the province of kabuki and were discouraged, over time, by the kyōgen actors.

The broad and often sharp humor of the seventeenth century texts contrasts strangely with the lilting flute closure which they favor. The *shagiri dome*, as it is called, is a short, lively piece during which the actor usually leaps from side to side, concluding with the cry "iya." Even those plays with a "chase off" closure have a flute ending as well. The musical closure seems to have contributed to a mood of reconciliation both for the characters and for the audience and was still in use intermittently in late Edo, as we can see from notes in the late-Edo *Kumogata bon* text of the Izumi school. This type of closure was important during the Edo period when kyōgen actors had to be particularly sensitive to their government audiences and to the preferences of the noh actors with whom they performed. The reason for the change to the "chase off" scene in later texts may have been to preserve the continuity of the play which seems to end abruptly when a flute closure is used. However, a more practical reason was that the musicians had to be paid extra to remain on stage for the kyō-gen and the change was therefore a financial expedient.[37] Today, the flute ending is limited almost exclusively to *waki kyōgen* (auspicious plays).

Other changes of a more general nature can be seen in the texts as well. The stock characters became better defined: their self-introduction scenes were made uniform and the verbal endings they use were made to reflect their status. The texts themselves became more precise, eliminating the scattered notes to the actor which can be found interspersed with the dialogue in early texts. Under the patronage of the Tokugawa shogunate, the kyōgen actors were able to refine their art along the lines of noh. The kyōgen language became a stage language and the once improvisational skit evolved into a classical comedy.

With the downfall of the Edo government the troupes most dependent on it collapsed as well. The Sagi school almost completely disappeared although remnants remain on Sado island. The head of the Ōkura school retired to the countryside. Only the Izumi school, at a geographic remove from events in the capital, continued intact. At the request of the new Meiji government it was invited to perform with noh at the Iwakura mansion in Tokyo in 1876 and in this way succeeded in establishing itself in Tokyo. Today, the Nomura, Miyake, and Izumi families of the Izumi school are located in Tokyo, although branch families still perform in Nagoya (Nomura Matasaburō) and in Kanazawa. The resurgence of the Ōkura family was thanks to the efforts of Yamamoto Azuma Jirō in Tokyo. Today, there are a number of active families in the Ōkura school. The Ya-mamotos and the Ōkuras are based in Tokyo. The main branch of the Ōkura school Shigeyama family is in Kyoto, while the Chūsaburō branch performs in Shikoku and Kyushu as well as Kyoto. The Zenchiku family, an offshoot of the Shigeyama Chūsaburō family since 1963, is located in Osaka.[38]

In contemporary Japan the kyōgen actors of each of the schools have adjusted to a new audience accustomed to the fast pace of television

and film. It is not unusual to flip on the television and see Shigeyama
Sengorō in a contemporary melodrama. Nomura Mansaku once appeared
in a coffee commercial and more recently in *Falstaff*, based on
Shakespeare's *Henry IV*. His son, Takeshi, has appeared as an extra in
films. The younger actors of both families have acted in experimental
performances of Beckett and contemporary drama. Some of the most interesting facets of kyōgen, however, are those which seem to date back to
differences between the schools in the Edo period. For example, if we
compare performances by three different families of the play *Buaku* we see
a very different attitude in each performance.

Buaku opens with the master calling out his servant, Tarō Kaja,
and demanding that he kill the delinquent servant Buaku. Tarō Kaja makes
excuses for Buaku but to no avail, and he is forced finally to go off in
search of Buaku with a sword in hand. He discovers Buaku and convinces
him to come fishing, planning to catch him off guard. However, every time
he is about to slice off Buaku's head, his would-be victim Buaku turns
around to chat with him. When Buaku realizes what is going on, he weeps
over this betrayal by his friend and then invites Tarō Kaja to go ahead and
behead him. Tarō Kaja begins crying as well and finally urges Buaku to escape. At this juncture the Nomura family (Izumi school) interpretation diverges from that of the Yamamotos (Ōkura school). In the Nomura version, the two part, forlornly, with Tarō Kaja gazing abjectly after his re-
treating comrade. In the Yamamoto version, however, just as Buaku turns
to go, the conscientious servant has a change of heart and, reaching for his
sword, starts after him. Tarō Kaja does not pursue Buaku but this gesture,
not written into the texts, is paradigmatic of the Yamamoto interpretation of
the play. Tarō Kaja's gesture is a physical expression of an inner conflict:
is he to be loyal to the man he serves, or to his lifelong friend? He chooses
his friend but he has second thoughts. This tension between feelings of
friendship or love on the one hand and loyalty to one's superior on the
other is at the core of most Edo period literature, particularly the plays of
Chikamatsu Monzaemon. The long tradition in the Ōkura school of aiming
to please the samurai class surfaces in the interpretations preserved by the
Yamamoto family. The mood is reinforced by the rigidity of the vocal
rhythm unique to the Yamamotos. Precisely because of the monotony of
the delivery they are able, with the slightest deviation in gesture, to give the
plays a unique dimension.

In a subsequent scene in the same play, the Shigeyama (Ōkura
school) family's interpretation is of special interest. After Tarō Kaja's return, the master insists on going to Kiyomizu temple to pray for Buaku's
soul. In the precincts of the temple, whom do they happen upon but Buaku.

Tarō Kaja grabs Buaku and hurriedly convinces him to return dressed as a ghost before the master gets suspicious. The Shigeyamas portray a fearful Buaku who must be repeatedly enjoined by Tarō Kaja. When he does return and comes face to face with the master, he panics and makes a flying leap for one of the pillars on stage, wrapping himself around it. This type of broad and seemingly spontaneous gesture is typical of the Shigeyama family, and not found in performances of the other kyōgen families. Although the Shigeyamas are in no way related to the Sagi school, one can see a kind of spiritual kinship in their easy adaptability to the audience.

In contrast to the Yamamoto and Shigeyama families, both of the Ōkura school, the Nomura family is closely linked to a tradition of humanism and realism which we see in the early Izumi school. In *Buaku*, it is most apparent in the scene in which Buaku confronts the master. Unlike the Yamamoto's master who is stern and disbelieving, the Nomura's master panics at the sight of the ghost. His mouth drops open, his arms go rigid at his sides with his fingers splayed. At first, Buaku too is fearful, but seeing how successful his costume has been, he becomes bolder and bolder, approaching closer and closer to the master. Tarō Kaja intercedes, trying desperately to keep the two apart lest the master recognize Buaku's trick. He gestures frantically to Buaku from behind the master's back but Buaku pays him no mind. The focus is on the psychological relationship between the two servants rather than on the master-servant bond.

Some of the differences that can be seen between the schools are really differences in the individual actor's style. For example, in the spring of 1980, Shigeyama Sensaku gave a charmingly earthy performance in Tokyo of the play, *Iori no ume* (Plum Blossoms), which so altered the tone that the play almost seemed an entirely different one than that performed a week earlier by the Izumi school actor, Miyake Tōkurō. *Iori no ume* is a *nohgakari* play. That is to say, it is one of a group of kyōgen plays which follow, in abbreviated fashion, the formal structure of a noh play: musicians remain on-stage, a dance is offered by the *shite* (lead character), and much of the play is in poetry. The shite is, in this case, an elderly nun who invites the maidens of the village to visit and compose poetry every year when the plum comes into blossom. As the play opens, the nun is hidden from sight in her hut (a prop often used in noh consisting of a bamboo frame and drapes). A group of maidens enters to *sagari ha* music (noh entrance music for groups of characters), and calls upon the nun. Each offers a poem which the nun ties to the branches of the tree: an elegant and refined party. Miyake Tōkurō, in the role of the nun, then performed a *komai* (a short kyōgen dance) with a delicacy in keeping with the elegant mood of blossom viewing. When Sensaku performed the piece a week later, however, at the close of the dance he turned his back to the audience and wagged his behind at them before sitting down. This coy touch, like the shuddering Buaku clinging to the pillar, breaks through audience complacency in the face of a stylized art form.

Kyōgen has survived not simply as a museum piece but as an active comic drama, still responding to the changing attitudes of the audience. Curiously enough the stylized format of the texts has helped rather than hindered the actor in his effort to bring the plays to life. How this is possible is the subject of the next chapter.

Buaku shivering in fear at the pillar (the Ōkura school version of *Buaku*).

The master freezes in fright at the sight of Buaku's ghost
(the Izumi school version of *Buaku*).

A coy old nun dances (Shigeyama Sensaku in *Iori no ume*).

III.
THE SHAPING OF THE TEXT: *THE CRAB*

In tracing the evolution of the kyōgen text we see a gradual movement away from remnants of the earlier oral tradition and towards a more defined dramatic performance. Plays in the earliest text, *Tenshō bon* (1570), for example, are simple plot summaries—often no more than two or three lines—to be filled in by the actors on the spot. Only songs, riddles, or proverbs essential to the plot are written out for easy memorization by the actors. During the seventeenth and eighteenth centuries, as the audience grew more sophisticated, the texts became progressively more coherent, and the plays were categorized by easily recognizable character-types. While never to become as highly structured as a noh play, the kyō-gen plays in texts from the eighteenth century onward are built on sequences of speech and patterns of movement which reappear throughout the genre. Whatever improvisation once existed is confined to subtleties in timing and nuances in vocalization. Changes in the form of the text were accompanied by, and often determined, changes in the content and tone as well. For the mountain priest plays this meant, most conspicuously, a change from humor dependent on a belief in the existence of evil spirits and magic, to an ironic and yet sympathetic look at the foolishness of man as epitomized by the mountain priest, an attitude which was to become the dominant tone of kyōgen.

The progression from oral tradition to written text and the changes this entailed can be understood by comparing the texts for *The Crab*, one of the oldest mountain priest kyōgen plays. *The Crab* was originally about a malevolent crab spirit and not about mountain priests at all. There is something disturbingly medieval about this anthropomorphized evil lurking in the gloom and roar of the mountains. It hints at a world out of control and haunted by the supernatural. The humor is the rough-edged and often violent humor of a world in chaos: the world of medieval Japan. The inspiration for the play appears to have been one of the popular medieval ghost riddle tales. In one version, a priest stops at a temple and in the middle of the night is accosted by a crab spirit with a riddle. "Little legs, eight; big legs, two; two eyes looking up to the sky, from side to side I move (what am I?)." The priest immediately recognizes it for a crab spirit and crushes its shell with his staff. The next morning, a large crab is found dead.[1] There is no comic element here, unless the very existence of a crab spirit is

41

perceived as comic; rather it is a simple recitation of purported facts, much in the manner of the *Nihon ryōiki* (a Buddhist collection of miraculous tales from the Nara period.) Although the wished for conclusion prevails, the tale still seems to confirm our worst fears of a world haunted by evil spirits. The humor of the later kyōgen version, on the other hand, lies in large part in the failure of the man to outmaneuver the spirit.

In the earliest version of the play in *Tenshō bon* entitled *Kanibakemono* (Crab Spirit), two travelers are stopped on their journey by a forbidding sky. A spirit appears, hovering in the shadows, and presents them with a riddle: "Two big legs, eight little ones, both eyes looking up to the sky, and a shell that slips over the ground (what am I?)." The travelers cry out, "It's a crab!" and are promptly seized by the crab's pincers. It hauls them back and forth by the ears before dragging them offstage.[2] First of all, we are not looking at mountain priests and this serves to focus our attention on the crab. Secondly, the crab is menacingly silent with the exception of the riddle. In this the atmosphere is similar to the ghost riddle tale mentioned above. Finally, the two do not escape, but are dragged off by the spirit. There is as much fear as fun in such a portrayal and disturbingly little hope for a fair battle with the elements, as represented in this case by the crab.

This kind of black humor seems to be characteristic of a society facing extremes, be they of a social, political, or climatic nature. For example, in the village performances of noh and kyōgen at Kurokawa in Yamagata prefecture we see unexpected variants of plays in the standard repertoire. The kyōgen *Tsurigitsune* (Fox Trapping) ends with a white fox being trapped and dragged offstage, unlike his counterpart in the orthodox performances who escapes unharmed. There is no satisfactory method for dating the Kurokawa plays, but the tough, uncompromising humor does seem to be a response to the harsh life in the snow country. This is the type of response that we see in medieval Japan as well where people faced a society "upside down" (*gekokujō*), in which the almost continual warfare could reverse a person's fortunes overnight. For similar reasons, the period of the Great Depression in the United States gave us such comedians as Laurel and Hardy, Buster Keaton, and Charlie Chaplin. As LaFleur points out in *The Karma of Words*, in kyōgen comedy good does not necessarily triumph over evil; rather, wit triumphs over innocence and stupidity.[3] Instead of the fanciful wish fulfillment of early tale literature, kyōgen plays are characterized by the success of the clever and the streetwise. The two travelers in *The Crab* are too innocent of danger and evil to avoid being trapped and humiliated.

The somewhat brutal and crude humor of *The Crab* in the *Tenshō bon* text is characteristic of the plays in this collection. In *Persimmons*, for example, a childlike mountain priest is trapped up in a persimmon tree, caught stealing persimmons by the owner. However, instead of one owner appearing, in the *Tenshō bon* text two owners appear to harass and humiliate the lone mountain priest.[4] Or, in *The Lunchbox Thief*, instead of one mountain priest praying against the thief, a whole troupe of mountain priests prays and then tosses him up in the air before exiting.[5] The only other instances of a group of mountain priests appearing on stage are in the noh plays *Tanikō* and *Ataka*. The effect of the chorus of incantations is intimidating to say the least. There is something alarming in the blunt, hard-edged humor of the *Tenshō bon*. Judging from the text alone, it is difficult to visualize what the plays must have looked like on stage. However, we probably would not be far wrong in imagining the rough and tumble humor of an early Laurel and Hardy film where part of the thrill consists in being frightened by the foolish antics of the pair.

A group of mountain priests praying in unison (the noh play *Tanikō*)

With later refinements to the text, *The Crab* lost some of its eeriness and, in the Ōkura and Sagi school texts, a certain rationale was supplied for the appearance of the spirit. The assumption of the existence of a crab spirit intersecting our everyday plane of existence became the stuff of play and fantasy. In the Ōkura school *Toraaki bon* text (1642) the two travelers are now two priests (*kyakusō*). The description of the crab's manifestation is left out but when the crab does appear, it speaks and explains its presence. It has manifested itself in order to test the powers of the priests who have been bragging to one another. "Since you've been bragging so much about your powers, I came out to see for myself." The crab pinches one of the priests by the ear and the other priest threatens him. "If you don't let go, I'll pray that the Guardian King lassoes you in his rope and then I'll pray you dead. Do you still refuse?" The crab responds, "Let's see how good your prayers are. I'm not letting go."[6] We not only know why the crab has appeared—the hubris of the priests has brought him out—but it turns out to be a loquacious fellow quite capable of holding its own in verbal jousting.

The provision of a rationale for the crab spirit's appearance is intriguing. We no longer need feel threatened by the reasonless dangers of nature in a world out of control. We know exactly why the crab spirit has appeared to these two priests. The verbal exchanges, moreover, serve to undermine the menacing quality of the crab. It seems no longer to be a being from another realm intersecting ours, but rather the product of the fanciful imagination of two perfectly ordinary beings in our own realm. In other words, the play has become one about two foolish priests. This is supported by its conclusion. The crab drags the two offstage by their ears as in the *Tenshō bon* version, but here the exit is accompanied by a *shagiri* ending (a light, auspicious flute passage.) That is to say, the play is safely contained within the realm of performance and not allowed to intrude on our sense of reality. These changes in the play are consistent with what we would expect from the general trend in the *Toraaki bon* toward making the plays more coherent and dramatic.

Although the crab spirit is not so talkative in the Izumi school text, the *Tenri bon* (*Kyōgen rikugi*, 1646), the focus of the play still shifts markedly from the crab spirit to the priest and his companion. The two chat intimately about the porter's sister as they hike along and the mountain priest displays a decidedly unpriest-like interest in her, ".... very sweet! Tell her to come see me when we get back."[7] Later, they argue intensely over who should be the first to approach the crab, neither having the courage to do so. The intimate quality of the *Tenri bon* text, with its folksy homilies and scenes of everyday life, was meant to appeal to the commoners dwelling in and around the old capital of Kyoto where the Izumi school was centered during the Edo period.

Similarly, many of the *Tenri bon* plays include rather elaborate explanations much like the popular teaching texts (religious texts, correspondence texts, and folk tales) oriented toward enlightening the public.[8] In *The Crab*, for example, the riddle is repeated and discussed at some length before the mountain priest solves it.[9] We are drawn into the relationship between the bungling priest and his companion, with the crab reduced to a mechanism of the plot. The closure is even more graceful than in the *Toraaki bon* text. Here, the two are tossed aside before the crab exits to the notes of the flute.[10]

The texts from this period, the early seventeenth century, are clearly transitional between the oral tradition and a newly recorded textual tradition. While a structure for the plays has definitely emerged, there are still significant gaps in the plot. The *Tenri bon* is, in this respect, little better than the *Tenshō bon* which precedes it. Repetitive dialogue, too, suggests that the texts were jotted down from stage performances rather than being composed for the written page as later texts were. However, the very fact that the plays were formally recorded marks the beginning of a change in attitude toward the text and kyōgen theater as well. The tone is reflective of a new period and a new audience. Subtle differences between the texts of differing schools of kyōgen also suggest an emerging self-conciousness within the schools and families of kyōgen.

By the eighteenth century, the crab's precipitous appearance is given credibility within the context of the play. In the *Toraaki bon* version the crab makes an abrupt appearance. The backround leading up to the manifestation may have been improvised on the spot, but it is conspicuously missing from the text although Toraaki is meticulous about including comparable scenes in other plays. In *Tenri bon,* the travelers comment on the sudden darkening of the sky, but even in this case the later Izumi texts add more detail to the scene. In the *Kumogata bon* text the priest comments, "We're really deep in the mountains now. The sky's getting dark. It's creepy." And, further on, he cries out, startled, "Something's crying 'tō-tō'."[11] What is intriguing about the eighteenth century *Torahiro bon* text is that a name is affixed to the spot where the crab appears, Crab Swamp in the Province of Kō.[12] The specification of the place, also introduced with a slightly different name in the Sagi school texts, lends the play a more convincing stage realism and is rare enough in kyōgen to deserve our attention. In most cases, after all, proper names were deleted from the texts in order to make them more universally appealing. In *The Crab*, however, the setting is not just anywhere, it is Crab Swamp. The priests stumble onto a seemingly credible scene which then provides a startling contrast to the nonsense of the chatty crab. In other words, the play proceeds based on a false sense of realism which helps to make the plot more credible and therefore the confrontation more humorous.

On a more profound level, the play casts doubt on our perception of reality. What appears to be real, the play intimates, may prove to be quite unreal depending on the circumstances. Or, as Toraaki himself comments in his critical work, *Waranbegusa*, "Kyōgen makes the real unreal."[13] What seems at first to be an everyday scene with two priests hiking through the mountains and pausing at a place called Crab Swamp becomes highly unreal with the entry of the talking crab. While place names are an unusual feature in the later texts, the increasing preoccupation with realistic detail in both verbal descriptions and in the mime is what entitles kyōgen to be called "realistic theater," in spite of the highly stylized performances. On the other hand, with the abrupt introduction of an element of the absurd, the details of daily life seem to provide a venue for their own destruction by highlighting an altogether different reality exposed underneath.

Secondly, the use of place names establishes a link to medieval tale literature. Although Zeami had early on cautioned the kyōgen actors to base their plays on legends and amusing stories, this relationship is secured very late in *The Crab*.[14] The early ghost riddle link to the play in *Tenshō bon* is nebulous at best. In the *Tōkaidō meishoki* (A Record of Famous Spots along the Tōkaidō, 1660) we see a later version of the crab riddle in the context of a legend about a particular place. A traveling priest unravels the riddle of a spirit haunting Crab Slope in Ōmi province and puts a stop to the troubles thereby.[15] This entry in the Tōkaidō record is similar to the explanation given by Ōkura Toramitsu in his critical work of the early nineteenth century, *Kyōgen Fushinshi*. According to Toramitsu, a place called Crab Slope existed at the base of Mount Suzuka in Ise. A giant crab was said to have bewitched and injured travelers there until a priest destroyed it with prayers. The priest built a grave on the spot in memory of the crab.[16] The seemingly self-conscious selection of a name so similar to that in the tale, however, suggests an attempt to link the play to the legend. Why? After all, this connection is overtly drawn long after the potency of the legend had been lost and it had become just another innocuous folk tale. The most likely impetus would seem to be the kyōgen actors' desire—in particular the actors of the Ōkura and Sagi schools—to court the favor of the dominant noh troupes and thus receive the patronage of the Tokugawa elite. This might help to explain the absence of the place name in contemporary Izumi school texts. The Izumi school was not competing for Tokugawa patronage since it was located in the Kyoto area. Presumably, the noh troupes and, eventually, the samurai elite as well would have encouraged attempts to follow the tradition of developing plays based on folk tales, whether or not they were aware of the origins of the tradition in Zeami's secret treatises. In doing so, the actors could gloss over any evidence of social commentary in the plays. While satire of a mountain priest would have been unlikely to disturb the government, satire of other characters such as the daimyō and the master would. A trend toward removing potentially offensive satire extended over the genre as a whole during the Edo period, as we can see by comparing the plays in the *Tenshō bon* text with those in later texts of the Ōkura school.

The sensitivity of the Ōkura school to the Edo government is already apparent in Toraaki's critical work, *Waranbegusa*, from an earlier period.[17] His criticisms of the then-popular Sagi school, as well as his insistence on the proper way of performing, are indicative of his preoccupation with refining kyōgen for an elite audience, a refinement that was not accomplished until the eighteenth century texts and later. The style of performance which he advocates was appropriate to the intimate audience of the drawing room (*zashiki kyōgen*), and not to the large, outdoor stages where kyōgen was competing with kabuki for popularity. Although, unfortunately for Toraaki, the tastes of the government audience did not catch up with him in his lifetime, the style of acting that was to prevail was that promoted by Toraaki and the Ōkura school. By the time of the *Torahiro bon* text in the eighteenth century kyōgen had eliminated the improvisational element still apparent in the Sagi acting. The audience for kyōgen was the same as that for the noh theater and we may assume that the government elite had been educated to accept, and even to demand, a more refined form of comedy.

The kyōgen texts of the eighteenth century specify not only a place but a mountain priest and a mountain priest of a particular area as well. In the noh plays mountain priests are variously associated with the Kumano mountains, Mount Ōmine, Mount Hiko, and Mount Haguro, all of which were areas associated with mountain priests during noh's most active developmental period. By late Muromachi and early Edo, only Mount Haguro was regarded as a major center where mountain priests pursued their various disciplines, particularly magic and incantations. Mount Haguro thus becomes a useful rubric for anyone hoping to pass himself off as a powerful mountain priest. Predictably almost all of the mountain priests in the later kyōgen texts claim affiliation with Mount Haguro.

With the entrance of the mountain priest the text alters dramatically. Onstage, the mountain priest in his elaborate and colorful costume complete with black cap, white or orange cotton balls decorating his mantle, and an enormous conch shell hanging from his waist, dominates the stage. His gestures are large, and his bravado slightly intimidating. As in the instance of the specific place name, Crab Swamp, the identification of the mountain priest imposes a certain order on the plays. The priest is not just any priest; he is a mountain priest from Mount Haguro. He has become a character-type. The bragging and subsequent demise of the mountain priest is all the more humorous in that he has so clearly exaggerated his connections. The underlying reality which breaks through is that this supposed grand mountain priest is no different from one of us. This does not deny the possibility of the existence of the superhuman mountain priest; rather, the belief in such a myth provides for the revelation of the very human man who cannot live up to the myth.

While a certain amount of improvisation continued to be part of kyōgen performance in the seventeenth century, from the eighteenth century on the texts, and presumably performance as well, became increasingly stylized and codified. The structural patterns already in evidence in the *Tenri bon* text and in the *Toraaki bon* text were standardized, allowing for little variation. In addition to the underlying structural patterns—the self-introduction, the travel scene, the closure, and so on—patterns associated with particular character-types become more pronounced. These patterns are striking in the case of the mountain priest figure because of their close affinity with noh.

As is the case with other changes in the texts, the standardization of patterns of performance helped to determine the direction which the humor of kyōgen was to take. The sheer repetition of standard patterns creates an expectation in the audience as regards the character. By breaking a sequence of patterns, the actor can slip out of the character and seemingly—though not literally—nod familiarly at the audience. He may do this at specific and identifiable junctures in the text, or, as we can observe in modern kyōgen performance, simply through subtle alterations in timing and voice throughout. In this way, the actor seems to be conducting an intimate and ironic commentary on the character vis-à-vis the audience. For example, all of the incantations in the Ōkura school from the eighteenth century onward and in the Izumi school texts from the late nineteenth century break the mountain priest's incantation scene after a few lines. In *The Crab* the mountain priest solemnly intones in noh dynamic style,

> A mountain priest is called a mountain priest
> because he sleeps in the mountains.[18]

He spins around to his porter whose ear is clasped in the crab's pincer and demands in near normal speaking tones, "Splendid, don't you think?" His porter replies, "It seems splendid all right, but I'm in agony here!" The break in the incantation pattern allows the actor to vary the timing and alter his voice. He gives the audience the illusion that they are sharing in an ironic commentary on the character. This type of intentional ironic commentary which functions to create a feeling of intimacy with the audience is reminiscent of the mood found in popular literature of the Edo period. *Gesaku* (playful fiction) generates a similar ironic tone through asides to the reader, sketches, and wordplay dependent on an insider's knowledge of the changing fashions of the times. This is especially true when it takes a comic turn, as in much of the *kokkeibon* (funny book) genre. Even as the readership for *gesaku* fiction grew far beyond that of a select coterie, *gesaku* writers continued to give the reader the feeling that he was one of an inner group "in the know."

In kyōgen, improvisation which had once formed the basis for humor was later consciously built into the text through asides and produced on stage through the artistry of the actor. Some of these asides are already present in the seventeenth century texts but they do not appear with enough regularity or consistency to suggest a change in the humor.[19] We can see how this change came about by examining the most important of the character patterns for the mountain priest, the incantations. In the seventeenth century texts, large sections of the incantations have been lifted almost verbatim from noh. The presence of the incantations at all hints at the beginnings of the creation of the mountain priest character-type. However, unlike the incantations in later texts, those in the seventeenth century texts are strung together almost without pause, as we would expect from the mountain priest in noh. In the early kyōgen versions, serious incantations appear side by side with children's songs. The result is a clear parody of noh. For example, the main incantation for *The Crab* is taken from the noh play, *Lady Aoi*. In *Toraaki bon, The Crab* is the only play using it, suggesting that this particular incantation was already being phased out by the Ōkura school although it appears in a number of the mountain priest plays of the Sagi and Izumi schools. The incantation appears in the *Toraaki bon* text as follows:

> A mountain priest follows in the steps of
>   the Great Ascetic En.
> He climbs the peaks of Ōmine and Kazuragi
>   realms of the Diamond Mandala and the
>   Womb Mandala;
> Brushes aside the mountain dew of the seven treasures
>   with his tufted mantle,
> Worn to protect him from the filth of this world.
> *Chinaberry prayer beads.... these are not.*
> *They're just any old beads I've rounded up*

and strung together.
I shall now offer a prayer.
To the east, Go Zanze
To the south, Gundari Yasha
To the west, Dai Itoku
To the north, Kongo Yasha.
Boron, boron, boron, boron....[20]

Up until "Chinaberry prayer beads.... these are not" the prayer is identical to that which appears in noh. The succeeding lines in italics, referring to the prayer beads, are a parody of those which would follow in the noh chant, "'Sarari, sarari' with such sound / I shake the red wooden beads of my rosary."[21] The verse parodying the noh lines was later inserted into a variety of different kyōgen incantations. In modern performances, at least, the kyōgen actor pauses to hold up and examine the beads before pronouncing on them. The next five lines which constitute an appeal to the four protectors of the Buddha are identical to those in the noh as well. This brings us to the ubiquitous prayer, "Boron, boron, boron," which every kyōgen mountain priest, regardless of the text, chants to the rolling of his prayer beads. There is no consensus on the derivation of this chant. It is thought to be either the sound of the conch shell carried by the mountain priests, or possibly related to the mantra known as the Lesser Fudō which is associated with the universal buddha, Dainichi Nyorai.[22] Both the Lesser and the Middle Fudō spells appear in the *Lady Aoi* play and are a corruption of Sanskrit mixed with meaningless magic syllables. *Lady Aoi* concludes with the Hannya Kyō sutra: "They that hear my name shall get Great Enlightenment; they that see my body shall attain to Buddhahood." [23]

The Crab, on the other hand, concludes instead with a segment from a Buddhist version of a children's A, B, C song, the authorship of which is popularly assigned to the eighth century Shingon priest, Kūkai. It contains all of the symbols of the kana syllabary and was used to teach children their alphabet.

Iro ha ni ho he to	Scented with passion,
Chirinuru *wo waka* yo	Still the flower of our youth falls
	By the way.
Tare so tsune naramu	Who shall remain forever unchanged
Ui no oku yama kefu koete	Today we cross the mountain depths
	Of our uncertain lives
Asaki yume mizi	And dream no shallow dream
Eimo sezu	Nor are we possessed by delusion.[24]

The kyōgen actors end the prayer with the second line "chirinuru wo waka." Ikeda Hiroshi suggests that this is because "wo waka" is a homonym for the commonly used syllables that appear in mountain priest spells, *sowaka*.[25] The combinations of prayers and the parts of the original preserved from noh, vary with the school and with the play, but what we do see in the seventeenth century texts is a juxtaposition of nonsense and seriously intoned incantations taken from noh. The parody is unavoidable and seems to have been a source of humor in the seventeenth century. In later texts for both schools the incantations are broken up frequently by comments from the mountain priest to his attendant. Moreover, the content is altered so drastically as to constitute a distinctive kyōgen prayer.

The most popular incantation in later texts from *Torahiro bon* onward is a completely comic rendition of an incantation found in the noh play *Ataka.*

A mountain priest is one who follows in the steps
of the Great Ascetic En,
the living incarnation of the guardian king, Fudō.
The *tokin* is the crown of the five wisdoms,
pleated into the twelve karmic links of rebirth.
(*Ataka*)[26]

In the kyōgen version this becomes,

A mountain priest is called a mountain priest
because he sleeps in the mountains
(*Splendid, don't you think?*)
A tokin is a foot-long piece of cloth
died black, folded in pleats and popped on the bean,
and therefore called a tokin.
Irataka prayer beads, these are not,
they're just any old beads I've rounded up
and strung together. . . " (*The Crab*)[27]

Unlike the incantation from *Toraaki bon*, this version in *Torahiro bon* consists of a complete displacement of the content from the serious to the absurd. The relationship to the original becomes one of intellectual pleasure rather than dramatic humor, especially with repetition. Is it a parody? Yes. But the incantation now stands on its own as a comic pattern for the mountain priest. What is funny is rather to be found in the aside, "Splendid, don't you think?" which occurs midway through the prayer, rupturing both form and content.

What happens to parody of this type in performance can be understood better if we look at the aikyōgen refrain for the noh *shidai* (introductory chant composed of 7/5/7/5/7/4 syllables) chanted by Benkei in *Ataka.*

> Dressed in traveling robes with *suzukake* vest
> Dressed in traveling robes with *suzukake* vest
> Will our dew-drenched sleeves still have wilted.

The aikyōgen actor picks up the refrain:

> On my robe the suzukake vest is torn
> So what's the use of it?[28]

Benkei and his men wonder whether their sleeves have become so soaked that they have drooped, in spite of the fact that they are clad in the suzukake vest used by the mountain priests as protection from the mountain dew. The aikyōgen character's suzukake vest, on the other hand, is torn and therefore totally useless. As Koyama Hiroshi rightly points out, the kyōgen refrain does not evoke a humorous response from the audience.[29] The content is comic but the form contains it and prevents the content from disrupting the play. This is also the case in the performance of the kyōgen incantations: the humor is in the asides.

A desire to avoid too close a parody of noh was responsible, to some extent at least, for the change in the incantation scene from one relying on parody of noh in the seventeenth century texts to a more ironic humor dependent on interruptions and asides in the eighteenth century texts. The concern of the kyōgen actors over offending the noh actors does not become apparent until the eighteenth century and even later in the Izumi school. In fact, we still see in Toraaki's interval kyōgen text, *Ainohon,* unusual juxtapositions of kyōgen intervals and noh plays which were clearly intended as parody. The kyōgen play *Hikkukuri* (All tied up) for example, appears as an aikyōgen during the noh *Tomoe. Hikkukuri* is about a shrew whose henpecked husband begs for a divorce. Finally she agrees but demands some proof of separation. When her husband urges her to take anything she likes and leave, she slips a bag over his head and drags him off saying, "This is what I want."[30] Since *Tomoe* concerns the only woman warrior of noh, the mistress of Kiso no Yoshinaka, the insertion of *Hikkukuri* within the play seems a rather bald attempt at parody. This type of parody soon disappeared. By the eighteenth century the Ōkura school at least had so altered the incantations in the mountain priest plays as to render the parody of noh negligible to the humor of the scene.[31]

It is fair to ask whether the changes in the incantations were made with the noh in mind or whether they were simply part of Torahiro's overall effort to make the plays more consistently comic. Certainly a livelier production resulted. We do know, however, that an uneasiness over offending the noh schools affected the Izumi school as well. In the *Kumogata bon* version of the play *Mushrooms,* notes to the actors warn that too close a parody of the noh entrance scene in these plays could be offensive. The play is distinctive for an opening scene which parallels that in the noh play *Lady Aoi.*[32] The notes instruct us as follows:

> The above is a parody of the greeting scene in the noh play *Lady Aoi*, during which the aikyōgen calls on the mountain priest... This copying of the *Lady Aoi* greeting scene is not a traditional device. It seems to have been a sudden inspiration. It is, however, an accepted technique in kyōgen. Since it is rather discourteous to the noh *waki* actor, the *waki* melody may be omitted in delivery....[33]

In other words, by the end of the Edo period, the Ōkura school's efforts to define the humor of kyōgen had influenced the Izumi school as well. While the *Kumogata bon* version of *The Crab* uses the incantations as they are used in noh, the incantations are repeatedly interrupted with asides to the porter. By late Edo, the Izumi school's *Kyōgenshūsei* text and the *Sanbyakubanshū* text both conform to the incantations used in the *Torahiro bon* text. Once again, the humor is not in the parody of noh but in the interruption of a formal pattern. As the humor moved away from parody, it moved closer to irony and to the presentation of a universal character-type.

The story of *The Crab* does not end here. To pursue it further, however, we would have to rely on comparisons of performance. The written text for *The Crab* reached more or less its final form with the middle and late Edo period texts. Further changes, especially in postwar kyōgen, are dependent on individual interpretation by the actors—interpretation made possible by the earlier standardization of the texts. The play about a frightening crab spirit was transformed over the years into one about two bumbling mountain priests and finally, into a play about everyman's foolish pride and blindness to his own faults. Far from calcifying into a fixed classical form, kyōgen continued and continues to respond to its audience. In *The Crab* the naivety of the kyōgen mountain priest, like that of the servant Tarō Kaja, is disarming and prepares us to accept the actor's sympathetic portrayal with an indulgent smile.

IV.
THE MAN WITHIN THE MYTH:
THE MOUNTAIN PRIEST CHARACTER

Given the consuming interest in transformations in this period, the character of the mountain priest seems a natural choice for kyōgen. Through arduous training in the mountains, he was said to be able not only to exorcise evil spirits causing illness or insanity but to transform himself into a mythical *tengu* beast with a pointed nose or a beak and feathers, or even into a falcon. An account in *Taiheiki* (The Chronicle of Great Peace) describes a banquet attended by mountain priests who were also *dengaku* performers. The witness who observed them through a crack in the wall reports,

> None of the performers of either the main guild or the branch guild were human. Some had beaks exactly like falcons, while others were in various stages of human transformation. Watching the participants I realized that they were a group of *tengu* and that the footprints on the mats were those of birds and beasts.[1]

In *Uji shūi monogatari* (A Collection of Tales from Uji) one of the tales tells of a tengu caught atop a persimmon tree by a minister of state. The tengu tries, unsuccessfully, to pass itself off as a Buddha. Subsequently, the tengu falls to earth and all that is left is a dead falcon with a broken wing.[2] Based on stories like these, the tengu was said to transform itself into a mountain priest or a falcon in order to become visible to the human eye. It followed, at least in popular imagination, that the reverse might also be true, a mountain priest might transform himself into a tengu or a falcon.

The legends and myths that collected around the mountain priest made him of immediate interest to both noh and kyōgen actors. He is, in fact, one of the earliest subjects for kyōgen. *Ninheiji hondō kuyō nikki* (Diary of the Memorial Service of Ninheiji) (1352) records the following in a list of entertainments: "Number eleven, kyōgen: a mountain priest's incantation."[3] This is the first instance of kyōgen being cited by title or plot. The impersonation of the mountain priest was not limited to theater, however. In a 1416 entry in *Kanmongyoki* we learn that one of the members of

55

a procession of shrine musicians dressed himself up as a mountain priest to the amusement of the bystanders.[4] Or, according to a 1419 entry in the same diary, a large crowd was said to have gathered when a group of young courtiers dressed up as mountain priests for a festival on the outskirts of Fushimi palace.[5] No doubt the parade of mountain priests through the streets of Kyoto twice a year enroute to the Yoshino mountains excited the lay imagination.

The link between magic and the performer is so close that mountain priests themselves inevitably crossed over into the performing arts. Descending upon villages after extensive retreats in the surrounding mountains, they would accompany a display of their powers with various forms of entertainment. There is ample documentation of such performances in the northeastern regions of Japan. They consisted of a variety of dances and contests of powers: *yamabushi kagura* (a variation of ritual Shinto shrine dance), *yamabushi bangaku* (a martial style of dance), *yamabushi okina sanbasō* (a New Year's ritual performance central to both noh and kyōgen), *kenkurabe* (a contest of powers), and even yamabushi noh and kyōgen, variants of the standard repertory.[6] H. Byron Earhart's study of the Mount Haguro sect of mountain priests contains a description of a series of *kenkurabe* on Mount Haguro. For one of the contests, called *karasu tobi* (crow leap), he includes a photograph (plate No. 5), which suggests that the "crow leap" is identical to that performed by kyōgen actors in modern performances of *Sanbasō*.[7] In any case, the mountain priests through their travels in the northern areas of Japan helped to disseminate the arts of noh and kyōgen. The mountain priest became both performer and subject of performance, not unlike the blind biwa player and linked-verse poet, fellow travelers who appear in the kyōgen plays.

In spite of the evident delight which the lay population took in impersonating the mountain priest, there was considerable confusion over who he was. The mountain priests themselves contributed to the confusion by the secrecy with which they enveloped their practices. The lay person had to rely as much on myths and tales, such as those in the Uji collection, as on any factual reports. Detailed histories of the Shugendō sect to which the mountain priest ultimately belonged were not yet available in this period and, in any case, even if he were literate, the layman would not have had access to them. We will not discover, then, the origins of the kyōgen mountain priest in the complex tomes of the Shugendō sect. Instead, we must turn to the popular tales, historical records, diaries, and literature of the period in order to tease out medieval man's perception of the mountain priest. The mountain priest who emerges is the basis for the kyōgen character: a character redolent of myth and legend.

To create the mountain priest character on stage, the actor manipulates the expectations of the audience regarding the character. Over the years, audience expectations have been incorporated into performance patterns as well as into isolated gestures, and, of course, the costume as well. For example, traces of the falcon myth appear in the Ōkura school's version of the mountain priest's self-introduction. He rises up on his toes with his arms and chest thrust forward, looking like a tremendous falcon about to lift off in flight. Or, in the Izumi school, the mountain priest's "high-step walk" (*hakobi ashi*) gives the impression that he is climbing some invisible mountain. This walk is only shared by the demon character, a fellow frequenter of the mountain depths. An informed audience, sharing a common cultural backround, helps to promote the aura emanating from the mountain priest on stage. During the course of the play, the superhuman myth is shattered repeatedly, exposing a very human man within.

Before entering into an analysis of the performance patterns themselves, we need a clearer vision of the audience expectations regarding the mountain priest character. We get some sense of how the mountain priest was viewed from the scroll *Ippen Shōnin Eden* (Priest Ippen's Life) (1239) by Tosa Mitsunobu.[8] Here, the mountain priest is depicted in the familiar garb of the kyōgen character: a small cap, tufted mantle, and black leggings. In the same period, we see the earliest mention of mountain priests in diaries and literature. They are described as Buddhist ascetics, alternately called *hijiri* (hermit), *ubasoku* (ascetic), or *gyōja* (man of power) and were attached loosely to either the Shingon or Tendai sects of esoteric Buddhism. After a retreat in the mountains to perform religious austerities, the ascetic would reenter society endowed with powers to cure illness and exorcise evil spirits.[9] The author of *Diary of the Reign of Emperor Hanazono* notes that as a last resort a mountain ascetic was called to the emperor's sickbed but his efforts were too late to revive the emperor.[10] Lady Murasaki, in her diary, describes the frightening sound of the mountain ascetics' incantations at the bedside of the empress during childbirth.[11] Murasaki's most dramatic account of an exorcism by a mountain ascetic is a fictional one from *The Tale of Genji*. An ascetic is summoned to relieve the pregnant Lady Aoi of possessing spirits. The most tenacious spirit is revealed to be the jealous Lady Rokujō, a rival for Prince Genji's love. The drama of the scene, the fierce rumbling of the incantations, the terrible trembling of the medium, the strange voices that issue from Lady Aoi, inspired the rendition of this episode in the noh play *Lady Aoi*. Scenes from the noh play are subsequently parodied in the kyōgen plays *Mushrooms* and *Owls,* both of which involve exorcisms. Whereas in noh the mountain priest successfully ousts the spirit, in kyōgen he is either possessed himself (*Owls*), or so intimidated by the spirits that he is chased off stage by them (*Mushrooms*).

By the twelfth century the number of mountain priests had swelled, and they began to form groups around the practice of certain ritual austerities known as *shugendō*. One reason for the growth in numbers and the new visibility of the mountain priests may have been the changing climate of the times: the decline of the Heian Court and the rise of a society of warrior elites. Because of their itinerant lifestyle, mountain priests were not infrequently called on to serve as political messengers between feuding daimyō. The nun Abutsu-ni notes in her diary, *Izayoi nikki,* that she used a mountain priest to deliver a message for her.[12] In other instances, warriors would masquerade as mountain priests in order to travel freely through the mountains. *Gikeiki* (The Chronicles of Yoshitsune) provides a fictional but convincing account of Yoshitsune's retreat north disguised as a mountain priest along with Benkei and his men. Their narrow escape is the subject of the noh play *Ataka,* and the kabuki play *Kanjinchō.*

Outwardly, the mountain priest was perceived as a man of power, be it political, spiritual, or physical. The internal source of his power was to be found in the mountains. From ancient times the mountains were said to be the home of spirits, demons, and the dead. His passage through the mountain wilds was thus a passage into the spirit world from which he gained his powers. In the process of formulating a code of behavior, the mountain priest superimposed the symbols of his own esoteric Buddhist beliefs over earlier folk beliefs. Thus, Mount Kimpu in Yoshino came to represent the Diamond Mandala, the Kumano range the Womb Mandala, and Mount Ōmine, overlapping the two, was the symbol of their essential unity.[13] Later, Mount Haguro in Yamagata prefecture was revered as well for the severity of the climb. The boastful mountain priest of kyōgen invariably claims to have origins on Mount Haguro and to have completed austerities on Mount Ōmine.

Many of the traditions of the mountain priest stem from the prototype of the ascetic En no gyōja (the Great En), the alleged founder of the Shugendō order.[14] Pictured in iconography with a straw hat, pointed beard, and an iron staff with rings, he is often summoned by mountain priests at times of trouble. The noh play *Tanikō* depicts a troupe of mountain priests who pray in unison to the Great En.[15] According to the play, during the course of their climb, a young boy in their company falls ill and, in accordance with the harsh code of the mountain priests, they hurl him over the side of a cliff. Then, overcome with sorrow, they pray that he may be restored to them. Suddenly, through the curtains at the far end of the bridgeway, the fierce Zao Gongen, guardian deity of the mountain priest, appears and with him, the Great Ascetic En.[16] They rescue the boy from the valley depths and bring him back to life. There is no evidence that such a cruel code of conduct actually existed but the story does illustrate the popular belief in the extreme severity of the Shugendō code.

The various disciplines followed by the mountain priest were given credence in that they were practices originating with En. He is said to have retired to the mountains, lived on pine needles, and recited without ceasing the Peacock Sutra. These austerities enabled him to pass through the barrier to the spirit world and to obtain supernatural powers.[17] The three disciplines of the mountain priest, cold water austerities (standing under a waterfall), fasting, and the recitation of power words, all originated with En. In its most dire form fasting meant total abstinence or *danjiki*.[18] Predictably, the kyōgen mountain priest attests to having undergone danjiki.

Another practice of the mountain priest, his recitation of power words (mantra), enabled him to perform miracles. Usually the purpose of the incantation was to exorcise an evil spirit, but in some cases it was used for divination as well. Originally the succession of syllables in the mantra had meaning in Sanskrit but by the time they were incorporated into Shingon and Tendai Buddhist practices, they were devoid of any intelligible meaning. Each mantra is associated with a particular Buddha or Bodhisattva. The only one which appears in kyōgen today is the Lesser Fudō, the mantra associated with the universal Buddha, Dainichi Nyorai (Vairochana): "on abiraunken bazara datoban" which becomes in kyōgen the familiar, "boron, boron, boron."[19] The kyōgen actors allude to the Amida Mantra in one of their incantations, *Iroha*, the content of which is actually a children's song.[20] The model for the incantation scene is provided in noh. Incantations play a major role in a number of noh plays, *Aoi no ue, Dōjōji, Kurozuka, Danpū, Nomori,* and *Ataka,* among others. In each case the loud pulsating beat of the incantation is the highlight of the performance. There is little evidence in medieval records to verify what the mountain priest recited and when. The evidence that does exist is gleaned from references in *A Collection of Tales from Uji, The Tale of the Heike,* and the noh plays, the same sources as those for the mountain priest legends. We also know from a single reference in *Tamon'in Nikki* that mountain priests did indeed use hand signs and chanted incantations.[21]

In addition to the buddhist mantra, the mountain priest also recited spells, *dharani* (ju). The Great Ascetic En is said to have recited the Peacock Spell, from which he gained his powers. The spells are simply longer versions of the mantra, used for the same purpose. Finally, the names of divinities (*hōgo*) were invoked for their empowering qualities. The main deity of the mountain priests and the one most often mentioned by the kyōgen character is Fudō Myōō, one of the five guardian kings who guard the five directions around the universal Buddha.[22] His fierce visage and fighting stance for quelling evil probably appealed to the mountain priests. Another favorite was Zao Gongen, the rescuing deity in the *Taniko* play. We find the determined kyōgen priest in the *Toraaki bon* version of *Owls* calling up Fudō Myōō in his effort to exorcise an owl spirit:

> No matter how determined an owl spirit you may be,
> flying about possessing people here and there,
> if I pray that Fudō Myōō lassoes you with his rope,
> we will be set free. . .[23]

In keeping with the humor of kyōgen, his prayer backfires and he ends up hooting his way off stage as well.

One of the more interesting disciplines of the mountain priest, at least in terms of humor in kyōgen, is his use of a variety of secret hand signs, *mudra* (*ketsujin*), which represent the overcoming of evil by good. As is true of the incantations, the mudra were in themselves a link to the Buddha, and thus a path to enlightenment. In kyōgen, however, they are used specifically to exorcise evil spirits. The mountain priest in *Owls* makes, quite appropriately, the sign of the "crow," while in *Mushrooms,* he chooses the sign of the "eggplant." Neither proves effective. On the other hand, the mischievous mountain priest of *The Snail* performs a mudra which enables him to disappear from sight, to the consternation of those chasing him.

It is easy to imagine the awe with which the mountain priest was regarded by villagers, what with his fierce visage, strange incantations, and mysterious signs. Even more striking than these, however, was his costume. Originally designed for suitability to mountain life, the articles of clothing came to aquire a symbolic value in Buddhist terms. Benkei, dressed in disguise as a mountain priest in the noh play *Ataka* lists in an incantation the articles of clothing:

> A mountain priest follows in the footsteps
> of the Great Ascetic En,
> the living incarnation of Fudō Myōō.
> The tokin is the crown of the five wisdoms
> pleated into the twelve karmic links of rebirth;

A mountain priest performs the crow mudra (*Owls*).

the persimmon-colored suzukake
represents the nine-layered Diamond Mandala;
the leggings we wear are black
like the Womb Mandala;
treading the eight-holed straw sandals,
breathing out and breathing in,
we intone Ah and Un.
A mountain priest is a living Buddha
in this very body.[24]

Each separate piece of the mountain priest's garb was a sign of Buddhist enlightenment. The recitation was therefore an empowering act. In *Mushrooms,* the mountain priest attempts to invoke this empowering quality but his prayer only brings disaster.

A tokin is a foot-long piece of cloth
dyed jet black, crumpled into pleats,
and popped on the bean,
and therefore called a tokin.[25]

The items of clothing are the same as those of the noh priest but the content is displaced from the serious to the absurd.

At the same time as a mythology of the mountain priest's powers was evolving, its opposite began to surface as well, in particular in tale literature of the medieval period. Here we see the false mountain priest who tries to deceive innocent people, or the pretender who stoops to petty thievery. This false mountain priest was founded in the reality of the medieval period. Constant warfare had made it relatively easy for people to slide from one profession into another when it proved expedient to do so. Becoming a mountain priest and receiving alms was an acceptable way of making a living. If you were clever enough, you might even forego the training altogether. Kyōgen pokes fun at just this phenomenon in *Uozeppō* (A Fish Sermon) in which a man sets out to hire a priest and gets instead a cook pretending to be a priest. When asked to recite sutras, the priest begins to recite the names of fish and is scolded for his "smelly sermon."

In several stories in *A Collection of Tales from Uji,* we are presented with opportunistic or false mountain priests. In one, "How a priest put the magic incantation of the Bodhisattva Zuigu into his forehead," a mountain priest, begging for alms, displays his newly healed scar.[26] He claims that while others may cut off a finger or toe as a pledge to the Buddha, he has inserted an incantation of the Bodhisattva into his head. A retainer standing nearby laughs and accuses him of aquiring the scar when he was caught in bed with another man's wife and had his head slit open with a hoe. The mountain priest smoothly replies, "That's when I seized the opportunity to put it in." Everyone laughs and the mountain priest slinks off. In another tale from the same collection, we have the ribald story "How the Middle Counselor Morotoki investigated a priest's penis."[27] A mountain priest claims to have "cut off my earthly ties" and exposes himself to prove it. The middle counselor discovers his trick (a combination of paste and ingenuity) and the priest joins in the laughter.

An opportunistic priest appears as well in the *Konjaku Monogatari* (Tales of Times Now Past) (ca. 1100) in a story called, "The Rice Poop Saint."[28] An ascetic claims to eat nothing but pine needles just as the Great En did, but when a group of curious young courtiers investigate his privy, they find rice in the defecation. A secret hoard of rice is subsequently discovered hidden under the floor boards in the "saint's" rooms. The humor in these stories is very like that in the kyōgen plays. In other words, the kyōgen character is not simply a parody. He has his own prototype in the everyday life of the period. The teasing mountain priest of *The Snail* who pretends to a boy that he is a snail and then leads him hopping about to the tune of a children's song is not far removed from these stories. Although in the kyōgen plays the tricks are more often played for their own sake rather than for personal gain.

On the one hand we have the human face of the mountain priest: his activities, his prototypes, his powers, at least as they were understood by the layman. On the other, we have the mountain priest's legendary ability to transform himself. For the villager this meant that one could never be sure whether one was dealing with a mountain priest or with a tengu pretending to be a mountain priest. One of the bases for the connection which the layman made between the two appears to be the ambiguity concerning the mountain priest's duties. In two kyōgen plays in the *Tenshō bon* text, *Igui* (Igui, the Disappearing Boy) and *Owls*, the mountain priest acts as a fortuneteller using divining instruments. In a picture of fortunetellers from the period, we see a mountain priest lined up with men in Shinto robes. This confusion is cleared up in the early Edo period texts where the mountain priest of *Owls* recites an incantation instead of using divining instruments, and the mountain priest of *Igui* is changed to a fortuneteller. Nevertheless, the fortune-teller in the *Toraaki bon* version of *Igui* explains that his name is actually *Tengu zaemon*. Satake argues that the fact that tengu were known for their divining abilities would not have been lost on the audience in the seventeenth century.[29] We have then a complex relationship between the mountain priest and the tengu who seem to be linked by their divining powers which were really the province of the fortune-teller and not of the mountain priest at all.

By far the greatest influence on contemporary perceptions of the mountain priest-tengu transformation was noh, where the legends were dramatized on stage. In three of the plays, *Daie, Kurumazō* and *Kurama tengu,* the mountain priest of the first half is revealed to be none other than a tengu in the second, reinforcing the mountain priest-tengu legends already in popular circulation. Whereas in noh the wild beast is found to be hidden within the breast of man, kyōgen offers instead plays about frolicking tengu who behave very humanly indeed, or about the boastful mountain priest revealed in all his human weakness.

A tengu in its mountain priest transformation
(the noh play *Kurama tengu*).

A tengu (the noh play *Kurama tengu*).

The powerful combination of a wild beast hidden in a human heart is the subject of *Kurama tengu*.[30] The great tengu who appears in the latter half of the play performs a violent *maibataraki* (martial) dance, whipping his long hair about as he shakes his head and stamps. This is the same tengu who introduces himself in the first half in the guise of a lonely and lovesick mountain priest. The story is taken from *Gikeiki* (The Chronicles of Yoshitsune) and describes how the young Yoshitsune (Ushiwaka) is taught the arts of war by the Great Tengu of Kurama Mountain. According to the play, Yoshitsune, the son of the defeated Minamoto general Yoshitomo, visits Mount Kurama with a group of children from the rival Heike clan to view the cherry blossoms. He has been living with the children at a temple on the far side of Sōjō valley on Mount Kurama. While the rest of the children flee at the sight of the fearsome mountain priest, Yoshitsune remains beneath the cherry trees. The mountain priest is dismayed that the young boys have fled in fear when he meant them no harm. For his part, Yoshitsune, living among the sons of his enemy, is as lonely as the priest in his mountain solitude.

The exchange which takes place between them has about it the tenderly erotic overtones of the commencement of a love affair. This impression is heightened by the *kakeai* style of recitation, in which the lines are shared by the two characters and the chorus to create a feeling of communality. We might note here that mountain priests, as well as tengu, were said to kidnap young boys and make off with them to the mountains. In *Shasekishū* (A Book of Sand and Pebbles) (1287), a collection of Buddhist tales from the period, a young acolyte disappears from a mountain temple in Ise and weeks later reappears on the roof of the same temple. He recounts how he was taken by a tengu to visit his temple in the mountains. In *Kurama tengu* Yoshitsune will also be taken on a tour of tengu temples, but first there is a confession of love from the mountain priest:

> Mountain Priest: I didn't realize you were still here,
> as quiet as the cherry blossoms hidden in the ravine
> where not even the chirp of a cricket can be heard.
> I'm so grateful.

> Ushiwaka: Who could have known? Am I like the
> white clouds that rise and mix with others? How
> could you have known?

> Mountain Priest: Who shall befriend me? In Takasago—

Ushiwaka: not even the pines are friends of old.

Mountain Priest: Flocking crows—

Chorus: mock the sowing of seeds
and though no more than seeds
these words exchanged
give rise to grasses of love
encouraging worldly rumors.
Oh blossoming plum within your fence
do not turn away from an old man, obsessed.
For the blossoms there is
always the promise of spring.
For man, a friendship begins in one night
but who knows where it will end?
Without warning the heart is lost.
Chances of meeting grow rare
but the torment of love grows greater.
Alas! It is bitter![31]

The lovesick mountain priest later reveals himself to be none other than the magnificent Great Tengu of Mount Kurama, and he promises to return to teach Yoshitsune the arts of war. During his initial leave-taking, his tengu self steps forth as the chorus chants:

The mountain priest breaks through the vastness of Sōjō valley,
Treads the clouds and rises in flight,
Treads the rising clouds and flies. . . .[32]

The tengu returns dressed in the terrifying *obeshimi* mask with its long nose and menacing expression. He carries a large round feathered fan to represent his wings. The chorus describes his entrance:

Trailing on mists turning to clouds, he vaults over Sōjō
valley,
where the moon glows darkly over Mount Kurama
and shakes the peak.
Storm gales, shrill autumn blasts,
like the roar of a waterfall,
the sound of the tengu tumbling to earth.
Oh terrible![33]

A similar transformation occurs in *Daie*. A tengu appears as a mountain priest to repay a debt to a Tendai priest who rescued him when he was in a falcon manifestation. In kyōgen, however, the opposite occurs. We see this in the interval kyōgen (aikyōgen) for *Kurama tengu,* in which a group of junior tengu are summoned to test Yoshitsune's skill with a sword. The interval kyōgen forms a transition between the human and spirit worlds in the two halves of the noh play. The leader of the junior tengu arrives first and announces that he is a "leaf-off-a-tree" (*ko no ha*) tengu. That is to say, a tengu as powerless as a leaf in the wind. He then calls out his troops and cautions them regarding the task ahead:

> I've heard that Lord Shana (Yoshitsune) has mastered
> all the secret arts of war. Chaps like us won't take him
> easily.[34]

After some preliminary jousting among themselves, the others decide to get out while they can.

> Why are poor creatures like us waiting around to get hurt?
> Let's get out of here! Retreat![35]

The leader of the troop first taunts them and then, thinking better of it, he flees after them.

> Hey! Are you running scared? Are you running scared?
> Why should I be the only one left behind? Wait up! Wait up![36]

A kotengu (an aikyōgen actor in the noh play *Kurama tengu*).

The very human tengu in the interval prepares the audience for the emergence of the Great Tengu in the second half of the noh play. The tenderhearted priest is transformed into a wild creature with a startling mask and violent gestures.

The peculiar mix of human within the tengu in kyōgen is particularly striking in a second tengu kyōgen, *Mukoiri Tengu* (Tengu Groom). Although this play is no longer performed, it was originally used both as an interval play and as an independent play. The feelings of the young tengu bride are at once comical and endearing.

> Leaf-off-a-Tree Tengu Bride:
> (sung in noh style [*issei*])
> It was her beak just like her Dad's
> that made him want her for his wife.
> (self-introduction)
> I am a leaf-off-a-tree tengu from Mount Atago.
> It's a lucky day, today, so I'm going to be given away
> as a bride.
> I must hurry along.
> (travel scene)
> Leaving Mount Atago
> Leaving Mount Atago
> My heart leaps to the sky.
> I jump the puddles in the road
> And with my tengu retainers in tow,
> I arrive at the door hung with pines
> Where my bridegroom waits within.[37]

The succeeding actions are described in notes. We are told that she enters and exchanges ceremonial cups of wine with her groom and father-in-law, after which the chorus sings:

> The pleasures of the new bride,
> the pleasures of the new bride,
> to fight, to quarrel, to knock heads together.
> Locking arms and wrestling is good, clean, fun,
> but as for a couple of newlyweds,
> they dance and dance,
> and then bed down.[38]

The scene captures both the domestic and the tengu side of the nuptial night.

The mountain priest's relationship to tengu was well established in noh and in tales of the period. The link between the mountain priest and falcon is more tenuous. The tengu, of course, is closely identified with the falcon. In terms of appearance alone, the tengu is often pictured with the falcon beak and wings. In noh, the *obeshimi* mask may have either a long nose or a beak. The kyōgen mask for the junior tengu is most often the falcon (*tonbi*) mask, characterized by a large beak. As we have seen, references in tales and in the noh reinforce this connection. In one of the tales from *A Collection of Tales from Uji* cited above, the tengu falls from a tree and appears on the ground as a dead falcon. In the noh play *Daie* a tengu tells of being rescued by a priest while in his falcon form. If a mountain priest could turn into a tengu and a tengu could turn into a falcon, then why could a mountain priest not turn directly into a falcon? This appears to be the question which the mountain priest in the kyōgen play *Persimmons* asks himself before plunging to the earth. Caught filching persimmons from an orchard, the mountain priest sequesters himself in the branches of a tree. The owner immediately recognizes that he is a mountain priest but decides to have a little fun with him. Is it a dog? A monkey? No, no. It's a falcon. The mountain priest mimes each animal in turn until he reaches the falcon. The owner insists that he fly and taps a beat with his fan to encourage him. Flapping his arms up and down the mountain priest leaps into the air and falls with a splat. He turns on the owner:

> You dare compare me, a great mountain priest,
> to birds and beasts and even a hawk? I thought I
> must have turned myself into a falcon since we
> can do that at the height of our powers. But I
> tried to fly and it seems my wings hadn't grown
> in yet. Because of you I fell, splat.[39]

In performances today the focus of the humor is on the various animals which the mountain priest mimes. Originally, however, if we refer back to the *Tenshō bon* text, only the falcon is mentioned. This version is very close to a tale in *Jikkinshō* (a collection of short tales) (1252) entitled, "An Awful Fall."[40] A mountain priest is so sure that his diet of pine needles has made him immortal like the Great En that he attempts to fly from a cliff. When he falls in a crippled heap the spectators burst into laughter. Similarly, the kyōgen mountain priest is so gullible that he succeeds in fooling himself into believing that he has become a falcon and can fly.

A mountain priest pretending to be a falcon
(Nomura Mansaku in *Persimmons*).

We now have a general impression of how the mountain priest was pictured by the commoner in the medieval period. He was summoned to bedsides of the ill and sent on secret missions by warring daimyō. Villagers shied away from him when he made a sudden appearance after a mountain retreat, afraid that what stood before them was not a man but a tengu. On the other hand, many of the mountain priests were not men of great powers at all but simple fellows trying to make a living and survive in a less than secure world. The possibility of attaining supernatural abilities through harsh ritual was never questioned. Certainly the mountain priest of *Sacroiliac* starts out full of confidence in his powers. Not everyone was capable of acquiring such powers, however, and those who failed or who only pretended to have mastered them were fair game for kyōgen.

In only two of the mountain priest plays do the mountain priests come out ahead: *The Snail* and *The Lunchbox Thief*. *The Lunchbox Thief*, at least the version performed today, is really a play about a thief. The mountain priest is the straight man. Although the patterns associated with him are the same as those used in other plays, the comic asides belong to the thief. In fact, in *Toraaki bon*, *The Lunchbox Thief* is not categorized as a mountain priest play; the lead role (*shite*) is given to the thief. In any case, the unbridled success of the mountain priest's incantation affords us a different perspective on the mountain priest. Clearly he is not the object of humor. In *The Snail* the mountain priest is a rascal who acts as a kind of Pied Piper, leading a young boy down the road to the hypnotic beat of his fan. He hops, skips, and cavorts about the stage with the mesmerized boy in tow. When the boy's father appears, far from giving up the hoax, the mountain priest ensnares the father as well. But the powers he uses are a game—a children's song about snails. The vulnerability of the boy and his father are not dependent on any supernatural powers. They are simply gullible and the mountain priest obliges them with a wild goose chase. In other words, it is gullibility and naivety in any form which are ridiculed and not the mountain priest in particular.[41]

In creating the mountain priest character, the actor first builds an atmosphere of power and legend around the mountain priest and then repeatedly dismantles it to reveal the man within the myth. We can better understand how this is done by looking closely at the performance patterns in *Persimmons*, a play about transformations and miracles. In the early versions, within the scope of one play the mountain priest both fails and succeeds in the exercise of his powers. Only by allowing for the belief of medieval man in the possibility of achieving such powers can we understand this seeming contradiction. The same mountain priest who fails to transform himself into a falcon succeeds in trapping his tormentor with his prayers. The powers are real but the mountain priest's facility with them is not. Interestingly, in modern performances the owner of the orchard only "pretends" to be trapped by the mountain priest's prayers, a concession to modern sensibilities.

There are five main performance patterns associated with the mountain priest, only two of which are generic to kyōgen, the introduction and the travel scene. Two, the shidai and the incantation, are indebted, to one extent or another, to parody of the mountain priest as he appears in the *waki* (secondary) role in noh. The fifth pattern is taken from a poem recorded in a collection of comic *haikai* (linked verse), *Inu tsukubashū* (1539) by Yamazaki Sōkan. In *Persimmons*, the mountain priest is carried forward through three consecutive performance patterns: the *shidai* (opening chant), the *nanori* (self-introduction), and the *michiyuki* (travel scene). The shidai, a musical and poetic form, is borrowed from noh where it is usually recited by the waki upon entering the stage. It consists of three lines of 7/5 7/5 7/4 syllables and is sung in the dynamic mode. The last line is taken up as a refrain by the chorus. In kyōgen the shidai is sung by the mountain priest, the demon, and the *shite* (main character) in *nohgakari* pieces. Normally the mountain priest is not accompanied by a chorus or musicians. The gestures are exactly those of the noh waki actor except that they are broader and more abrupt. Because the formal qualities are strictly adhered to, the kyōgen shidai is not comic in spite of the humorous content.

In a typical noh shidai from the play *Nomori* the waki mountain priest enters and sings to musical accompaniment:

> Drenched in the dew of moss, these sleeves
> Drenched in the dew of moss, these sleeves
> Where the jewel of enlightenment lies hidden.[42]

The shidai dramatizes the hardships of travel with reference to the dew-drenched sleeves, an allusion also to tears. The dew on the sleeves is compared to the jewel of enlightenment which lies hidden in the hearts of men and thus to the holiness of the priest's vocation. The contrast with the most typical kyōgen shidai is striking. In *Persimmons* the kyōgen mountain priest sings:

> A mountain priest with no conch shell to toot
> A mountain priest with no conch shell to toot
> Blows lies along his route.[43]

The tone is light and the content irreverent. Moreover, each of the three lines contains a pun which adds to the intellectual humor of the verse. In the first line, "kai wo mo motanu yamabushi wa," *kai* can refer either to the conch shell carried by the mountain priest as part of his gear, or to commandments. It has the alternative translation of "a mountain priest who keeps no commandments." The final line, "michi, michi, uso wo fukō yo," contains a pun on "*uso wo fuku*" which can mean either "to tell lies" or "to whistle." In the above translation I have chosen to give the interpretation which would be most immediately apparent to the audience. However, as the final line is repeated in a refrain with a slightly different intonation, the audience is given a pause in which to recognize the puns. Nevertheless, the shidai does not provoke laughter in the audience. By dint of constant repetition in association with the kyōgen mountain priest, the shidai has become a convention of the character. In most cases it is doubtful that the spectators are even aware of the puns, so accustomed are they to the shidai form.

The mountain priest goes directly from a typical shidai to a typical self-introduction with no break in the movement. He turns, takes two steps forward to the introduction position, faces the audience and announces:

> I am a mountain priest from Mount Haguro in Dewa.
> I've just done death-defying rites on Ōmine and Kazuragi
> And now I'm going home.[44]

A mountain priest performs a name announcement pattern
(*The Crab*).

There are variations on this introduction as can be seen by glancing through the plays, but all follow directly on the shidai and all exude the braggadocio identified with the character. By itself the introduction may not strike us as particularly amusing, but, following upon the absurdity of the shidai, the subsequent proclamation of "death-defying rites" is given a humorous cast. The bravado is implicitly denied, although here again the pattern is not expected to elicit laughter.

From the self-introduction, the mountain priest proceeds to the travel scene. The content of the travel scene for *Persimmons* is intentionally low-key in order to set off the "praying down a bird" scene which follows it:

> What's the rush? I'll just stroll along.
> (begins to circle the stage)
> I tell you, we mountain priests undergo such terrible
> death-defying rites that I now have great powers.
> I can do anything.

The travel scene signals a gradual increase in the complexity of the patterns in terms of the coordination of speech and gesture which are synchronized. The series culminates with the highly mimetic "praying down a bird" scene.

The "praying down a bird" scene is derived from a humorous verse in *Inu Tsukubashū*. The original is as follows:

> After staring at the sky
> from which however hard he prays
> no birds fall,
> the mountain priest goes out
> armed with bow and arrow.[45]

While at one time, the kyōgen audience might have been expected to supply the image of the failed mountain priest from the poem— haikai verses were part of popular culture in the fifteenth and sixteenth centuries—today's audience could not be expected to complete the allusion. In kyōgen the bird pattern includes both speech and accompanying mime. The actor concludes the travel scene as he heads toward the shite pillar. He draws out his words as he swings around to face the audience, "I have great powers." He then looks into the audience, "Why, just like that, I could pray a bird out of the sky." On the words "pray a bird," he looks up sharply to the roof edge on the stage and jerks his head rapidly from right to left and back up

A mountain priest performs the "praying down a bird" pattern
(Nomura Takeshi in *The Snail*).

to the center edge to mime the flight of the bird. On "out of," he turns his body slightly to the right and raises his left leg as well as his left hand grasping the prayer beads. On "the sky," he suddenly thrusts down his hand, foot, and head as if watching the bird plummet to earth. He is completely absorbed in the mime. Suddenly the tempo alters and he looks up, satisfied, and declares, "This time, the retreat has taken so long that I feel lucky to be going home in one piece." And, then, altering his tone altogether, he whines, "Oh dear! I haven't eaten since morning and I'm really hungry." The sudden change of mood from the intense control in the succession of patterns leading up to and culminating in the "bird" scene, to the whining complaint about his hunger, creates a caesura. The actor projects his own persona through the caesura and enjoys with the audience a momentary ironic view of the "would-be" mountain priest whose main preoccupation seems to be his stomach.

The single most important pattern for the mountain priest is the incantation scene which is adapted both metrically and in terms of stage movements from noh. In *Persimmons*, the mountain priest prepares his beads and, reaching into his repertory of spells "successfully" draws the re-treating owner back. The strict form of the prayers suggests real power in the mountain priest. The first prayer is based on a similar prayer in the play *Dampū*, where it is used by the mountain priest to pray a boat back into the harbor. The first two lines are identical but the remainder are rendered comic:

> Parting the clouds at the peak,
> piling up years of merit from rites,
> one meal a day, total fasting,
> standing rites, sitting rites,
> this great mountain priest entreats
> En the Ascetic and
> all of the gods and all of the Buddhas
> to please come to my aide with all of your powers.
> I roll my tightly strung *irataka* beads
> "clackety, clack" in my hands and
> I offer up this prayer.
> Boron, boron, boron, boron.[46]

The owner becomes "frantic" (or at least pretends to) when he finds himself trapped in the web of the prayer. At this point the mountain priest begins a second prayer. Whereas the first prayer followed the tone of the original in general, the second is taken from a popular children's song of the period:

> Irises under the bridge.
> Who planted the irises?
> It is I who planted the irises.
> Boron, boron, boron, boron.[47]

Both prayers are based, formally, on noh. However, in terms of performance they do not elicit laughter such as we would expect of parody. Instead, the break at the end of the prayer and the mountain priest's change of attitude allows the actor to step through and reveal the common man within. When the owner begs for mercy, the mountain priest, pleased with himself, asks, "Let you go?" An illusion of spontaneity is produced by this seemingly accidental aside and it is here that the audience laughs.

In each of the mountain priest plays a comic character type of the mountain priest is projected through the formal character patterns: the origins of the mountain priest in the mountains, his hardships, and his powers are all suggested in his costume, gesture, and speech patterns. The content of the performance patterns and the manner in which they are manipulated by the actor differ from one play to the next. In each instance, however, laughter occurs at the breaks in the patterns and not in response to the content of the patterns themselves. The actor, using his own stage persona, steps forth when there are breaks in the patterns, and in near normal speech and gesture shows us the ordinary man underneath the costume. In this respect, the mountain priest character is no different from any other character in the kyōgen repertory. In each case, when the character is dismantled, an ordinary man peers out at us, someone very much like ourselves.

V.
CONCLUSION

When kyōgen was primarily performed at local village shrines or at subscription performances in and around the old capital of Kyoto, a villager on his way to gather firewood might well have run into a mountain priest. When the mountain priest rushed past, eyes glittering and hair flying, the villager might have wondered whether what he had just seen was a man or a wild tengu. There is an expectation of the mountain priest's powers in the late sixteenth and early seventeenth centuries that puts an edge on the humor in the plays. The depiction in the sixteenth century text for *The Lunchbox Thief* of a group of mountain priests praying at a thief until he is paralyzed and then tossing him up in the air is as frightening as it is funny. In *Owls,* the failure of the mountain priest's prayer to exorcise the owl spirit leaves us with a certain uneasiness and foreboding. By the eighteenth and nineteenth centuries, kyōgen was primarily performed for city dwellers and the government elite in Edo and in Kyoto. When the city dweller did run into a mountain priest in the streets, he must have seen a rather scruffy, unimpressive-looking fellow, and the mountain priest's pretentions to power must have seemed, if anything, slightly absurd. The excitement of satirizing a mountain priest was dulled by his loss of prominence in society. The change in audience over time brought about a corresponding change in humor, not only in the mountain priest plays but in the genre as a whole. In order to continue to attract their audience, the actors sought to bring out the universally appealing aspects of their characters. As we saw in the text of *The Crab* and in the performance analysis of *Persimmons,* the actors are able to reveal the very human weaknesses of their characters by projecting their own persona through the characters at appropriate moments in the plays.

The dual relationship of the actor to his role and to the audience is a complex one in any dramatic form. In kyōgen we have neither the clear asides to the audience in which the actor steps out of character as in, for example, the role of Puck in *Midsummer Night's Dream,* nor do we have a complete identification with the role such as we find in the Stanislavsky method of Western realism. Perhaps a few comments by the actors themselves will help to clarify the actor's own perception of his role.

During a conference, "Ritual and Theater," at the Japan Society of New York in 1982, the kyōgen actor Nomura Mansaku was asked, "When

do you enter the role?" The question betrayed a western orientation to theater not strictly applicable to stylized dramatic forms. Mr. Nomura reacted
with bewilderment and then replied with pride, "My father, Manzō, once
said, 'I am always Nomura Manzō. Whether I perform the character of a
great lord or of a servant (Tarō Kaja), I am always Nomura Manzō.' " In
fact, the presence of the actor's persona within the role is essential to
kyōgen performance. Nomura Mansaku makes the point again in an
interview regarding the use of masks.[1] We are told that the noh actor dons
the mask and thereby empties himself of his personality and becomes the
role. In kyōgen, when masks are used, and this is a rarity, the actor's own
personality must be projected through the mask.

   Just as Charlie Chaplin and Buster Keaton are always themselves
no matter what role they play and yet we do not expect that they behave the
same way in their private lives, so too the kyōgen actor projects a stage
persona. Whereas the Chaplin persona is Chaplin alone, the kyōgen actor's
persona embraces the history of his family; the movement and voice are his
cultural and personal legacy. For the informed audience the projection of
the actor's familiar stage persona contributes to the intimacy of the kyōgen
acting style which at its best is almost a silent conversation between the actor and the audience. Because the audience must recognize the signs of the
character type, the audience role is one of active involvement. The
audience is necessary for the comic character to emerge in all his
dimensions and for the various components of parody, myth, and legend to
coalesce onstage in an autonomous figure.

   The essence of kyōgen humor lies in the unique communication
that arises between the actor and audience. For this communication to occur, the actor's stage persona must be allowed to slip through the character.
The communication which then results sets up an ironic relationship between audience and stage by means of which the actor and audience
become knowing onlookers regarding the characters who are fated to
stumble and fall as they are propelled forward by the mechanism of the
plot. Laughter arises when the rigid and stylized performance patterns
break and the actor is able to engage the audience in an ironic exchange.

   The actor's careful engagement of the audience helps to explain
why plays about the blind-man character are lightly humorous rather than
cruel, and why the mountain priest is still as much a figure of fun as he was
centuries ago. We do not laugh at the blind man but at the blind man in
each of us. The mountain priest in *Mushrooms* is humorous not simply
because he is a mountain priest who fails in his powers but because his
timidity and cowardice in confronting the mushrooms strikes a chord in the
audience. The kyōgen actor, in pointing out and laughing at the universal

weaknesses of the character, be they greed, pride, naivety, or simple cowardice, is teaching us to laugh at those same failings in ourselves. In the final analysis kyōgen is about us and our common humanity.

Part II: The Plays

PREFACE TO THE PLAYS

The translations that follow are based on the mountain priest plays as they appear in a late Edo period handwritten text for actors of the Izumi school. The text, popularly known as the *Kumogata bon*, was edited by Yoshida Koichi and published in the *Kotenbunko bon* series as the *Izumi ryū kyōgenshū*, twenty volumes, in 1955. This is not the final version of the plays as we see them today, although it is very close. In any case we would be precipitate in claiming any written text as a fixed version of a performance. In fact, the plethora of notes to the actors in the *Kumogata bon* text suggests a greater margin for interpretation than might otherwise be surmised from the extent of stylization in this and other texts of the period. The notes reflect the working attitudes of the actors of the period and as such have been much prized by scholars. The text has the feel of an artist's sketchbook out of which a performance might be created. Like texts in other popular genres of the Edo period--gesaku fiction, for example—or the scripts for kabuki plays, notes and asides as well as sketches are scattered throughout the text, making translation difficult. In order to preserve the notes and to make the translations clear, I have relegated the "notes to the actors" to footnotes. I have differentiated them from my own footnotes by placing them in brackets and indicating they are, "Notes to the Actor." In so doing I have sacrificed much of the rawness of the original text. My aim, in any case, has been to present the plays in a readable form.

Frequently the editor offers more than one possible alternative ending for a play. I have put these endings in footnotes for the reader's reference. They are significant in that today's actors sometimes choose one of the less conventional endings to alter the mood of a play. Moreover, the variety of endings attests to the flexibility of kyōgen.

Although kyōgen plays consist of many repetitive and formulaic expressions, the overall tone is informal and intimate, and I have therefore chosen to render the dialogue in as colloquial a style as possible without misrepresenting the original text. I have made no attempt to retain the intonation patterns peculiar to kyōgen vocalization which would have resulted in a stilted English style. When delivered by experienced actors, kyōgen has a natural flow that emerges out of the fixed intonation patterns, and I have tried to capture this in the dialogue of the plays. For poetry and prayers, I have used a formal style more suited to the stylized manner in which they are delivered.

Eight of the nine plays in the mountain priest category are presented here. The ninth play, *Inu yamabushi* (The Dog), is not included because it is almost identical to the play *The Shinto Priest and the Mountain Priest*. Moreover, probably because of the similarity of the two plays, only the second half of *The Dog* is recorded in the *Kumogata bon*. Both plays portray a rivalry between a Shinto priest and a mountain priest, and conclude with a prayer duel. In the one case, they pray to a dog, and in the other, to a Daikoku statue.

The costumes and props that appear at the opening of each of the plays are taken from the *Kumogata bon* text and therefore are not necessarily identical to what one would observe in a modern performance. Sometimes, for example, the directions instruct the actor to wear his hair "loose." This reflects the style of the Edo period when men customarily wore their hair long and tied up in a topknot. Hair worn down or "loose" would appear unkempt and more appropriate to a mountain man. For the most part, however, the mountain priest costume as described is what we would expect to see on stage today.

A glossary of kyōgen terms used in the plays is provided after the endnotes.

The Crab

THE CRAB[1]

Characters

Shite: Mountain Priest. Dressed in a brocade robe with geometric designs; kyōgen hakama bound to the knees; a three-quarter length travel cloak with broad sleeves in silk or gauze; a black, pleated cap; a mantle studded with tufted white or orange cotton balls; a large sword rather than a small dagger; a fan; prayer beads.[2]

Ado: Porter. Dressed in a striped robe with kyōgen hakama bound to the knees and a low narrow belt. His hair is loose with a small beret on top. He carries a conch shell hanging from his right hip and a travel chest strapped to a wooden staff.[3]

Ado: The Crab. Dressed in a mask, black cloth wig, and a large straw hat worn under a jacket to look like a shell.[4]

(Entrance music: noh flute, hip drum, shoulder drum)[5]

Priest   *(enters after two or three notes from the flute and marches down the bridgeway lifting his legs high as if mountain climbing. The porter follows him on stage.[6] The mountain priest proceeds to the waki spot and then makes an inward circle of the stage back to the shite spot. The porter follows him to the shite spot where they face each other and sing the shidai.)*

shidai (noh style)

    On his way down from the three peaks
    On his way down from the three peaks
    A mountain priest is grand indeed.

Porter   *(steps back and falls to one knee)* Grand indeed.

Priest   I'm a mountain priest from Mount Haguro in Dewa. I've just done death-defying rites on Ōmine and Kazuragi and now I'm headed home. Hey, porter! Where are you?

Porter	(*stands and faces him*) Sir!
Priest	You're here then?
Porter	(*kneels on one knee*) Before you, sir.
Priest	Well, stand up.
Porter	Yes, sir.
Priest	How about it? Even though we've been through endless, treacherous rites, we've made it through in one piece and we're on our way home. What could be better?
Porter	As you say, sir, what could be better?
Priest	(*begins to circle the stage*) Well, come along. Let's be off.
Porter	(*follows the priest*) Yes, sir.
Priest	We're lucky we made it down safely, this being your first try at the peaks.
Porter	It's all due to you, sir. I've never been so lucky before.
Priest	Your mother will be pleased to see us.
Porter	She certainly will, sir.
Priest	Which reminds me. Who's that girl your mother sent after us, asking me to look out for you?
Porter	Oh her. She's just my little sister, sir.
Priest	Who? Your sister?
Porter	Yes, sir.
Priest	Well, well, is that so? She looks nothing like you. Very sweet. Tell her to come see me when we get back.

Porter	Thank you, sir.
Priest	You know, as a rule, we don't talk about our mountain training, so if anyone asks, just say that it's scary.
Porter	I see, sir.
Priest	Oh yes, and you should learn a few prayers and incantations.
Porter	Yes, sir. Thank you, sir. But someone like me can't hope to accomplish much, although, at least, thanks to you, I've tried.
Priest	It's not easy, I know. But if you try your best, there's no reason why you shouldn't be able to do it.
Porter	You know, sir, everyone admires your powers.
Priest	What's that? You say everyone admires me?
Porter	That's right, sir.
Priest	Well! Of course, they do. Now then, let's go! Come on! (*continues around the stage*)
Porter	(*following*) Yes, sir.
Priest	(*gazes at the metsuke pillar*) Hmm...we're really deep in the mountains now. The sky's suddenly gotten dark. It's eerie.
Porter	It is kind of creepy.
Priest	Well, at times like these, we mountain priests have to keep moving. Let's go! Come on!
	(*circles the stage and heads toward the bridgeway*)
Porter	(*following*) Yes, sir.

Priest	I just don't understand this weather.
Porter	It's very creepy, sir.
Priest	(*stops at center stage and pauses, listening*) Ho! Something's crying, "Tō-tō."
Porter	Sir! Sir!
Priest	Well, what is it?
Porter	Let's turn back right away.
Priest	What for?
Porter	I'm scared.
Priest	Wait a minute! If you're going to be such a coward, how will you ever be able to call yourself a mountain priest?
Porter	(*tugs on the priest's sleeve*) Sir! I can only become a mountain priest if I'm alive! Please! Let's go!
Priest	Don't be stupid! Hold on to me (*grabs the porter's sleeve*) and forge ahead!
Porter	Ohhh, sir! We'd be better off going back!
Priest	(*approaches the bridgeway*) It keeps crying and it's heading this way!
Porter	It's creepy!
Priest	(*faces the crab which has now sidled onto the bridgeway*) Look! Something's there! (*scared, he flees to the waki spot*)
Porter	(*flees after the priest, clinging fearfully to him*) There's something there!
Priest	What was it? I couldn't make head nor tail of it.

Porter	I don't know, sir. Haven't you ever seen anything like it before?
Priest	Never. I've been to the mountains many, many times, but this is the first time I've seen anything like that!
Porter	Whatever it is, it's wierd!
Priest	You go up and find out what it is.
Porter	Yes, sir. But, I can't do that.
Priest	What? Why do you think I brought you along? Go on, ask!
Porter	I can't do it, sir. Please, you ask.
Priest	Humph! What a coward!

(*Puts his hand over his sword hilt and, rattling the sword, huffing and puffing, he approaches the crab. On the bridgeway the crab moves its pincers in the air.*)

No! No! I shouldn't have to do this. It's my porter's job to carry messages to strange creatures like this.

(*Backs up and tries not to look scared but only succeeds in looking foolish and pushes the porter forward.*)

Porter	Maybe a porter is supposed to carry the messages but I'm too scared. This is a job for the Master. Please, sir! You ask! (*hurls the priest in front of him*)
Priest	Ah, ah! Idiot!

(*Clutches his sword hilt and though girded, is clearly frightened. Stops at the shite spot.*)

Hey! You there! What are you?

Crab	(*At the first pine on the bridgeway, sidles back and forth, left and right.*)
	Two eyes looking into space, One shell slipping over the ground, Two big legs and eight little ones, Left to right I travel around.
Priest	It spoke!
Porter	I don't get it. What does it mean?
Priest	Ah ha! I know! It's a crab spirit!
Porter	What? A crab?
Priest	Absolutely!
Porter	Well, well, what a giant crab! How on earth did you figure it out?
Priest	First it said, "Two eyes looking into space." Those are its eyeballs. (*looks over at the crab*) See, they're stuck up there.
Porter	(*looks up*) Very scary eyes! They're staring at us!
Priest	Then it said, "A shell slipping over the ground." That's that shell of his. The "two big legs" are those pincers that keep trying to grab us.
Porter	What enormous pincers!
Priest	The "eight little legs" are those small legs of his. "From left to right" is because he can only move sideways.
Porter	You're sure it's a crab?
Priest	Positive. It's a crab all right.
Porter	Well, well! We have nothing to worry about then. To

think a silly crab could have scared me like that! Where is he? Where is he? Out of my way! (*rushes ahead waving his stick in the air*)

Priest   What're you up to?

Porter   I'll crush its shell with my stick and chase it away!

Priest   Poor creature! Leave it be.

Porter   Don't be a coward! (*rushes to the edge of the shite spot; the mountain priest follows*) Hey! You there! Your crabbiness is getting in the way of this august mountain ascetic. Go away. If you don't, I'll crush that shell of yours with my stick! I'll crush your shell! Here I come!

              (*Turns on the crab with his staff but after flailing about, he loses hold of the staff and the crab grabs him by the ear.*)[7]

              Ouch! Ouch!

              (*The crab drags him by the ear out to the main stage in front of the shite spot*)

Priest   What's happened?

Porter   The crab's got me!

Priest   Well, of course he has. That's exactly why I warned you! See what happens when you won't leave well enough alone. (*approaches them, gingerly*) Hey, you! Let him go! Let him go!

Porter   Ouch! Oh! Ouch! Don't just talk, do something! Quick! He's going to rip my ear off!

Priest   (*looks upset and faces forward*) Dear me! This is pretty bad! What'll I do? Wait! This is the moment I've been waiting for. Hang on! I'll pray you loose.

Porter   Hurry! Pray! Ouch! Oh! Ouch!

incantation (noh style)

Priest   (*Faces crab and chants in the dynamic mode.*)

                      Hear this!
                      I have undergone the harsh training of En the Great,
                      I have climbed the three peaks,
                      and piled up merit from years of training.
                      If such a great master as I prays,
                      your life will be in my hands.
                      I have strung together these irataka prayer beads.[8]
                      I roll them, "clackety, clack," (*rolls beads*)
                      and offer a prayer (*faces crab*)
                      Boron, boron, boron, boron. . [9]

Porter   Ouch! Ouch!

                      (*He is yanked out to center stage by the crab.*)

                      Sir, sir! He pinches harder with each clack. Ouch! Oh!
                      Ouch!

Priest   (*more and more distraught*) Oh this is awful! Hold on!
                      Hold on! I'll try praying at the pincer on your ear.

Porter   Who cares! Just get it off me!

incantation (noh style)

Priest   (*Circles the stage to the metsuke pillar. Passing in front
                      of the crab he makes a large mudra and claps his hands*)

                      No matter how crabby a crab you are
                      I'll make the blowing sign and chant,
                      "i-ro-ha-ni-ho-he-to" etcetera
                      "chi-ri-nu-ru-wo-waka," etcetera, etcetera,[10]
                      Boron, boron, boron, boron. . .

Porter   Ouch! Oh! Ouch!

(The crab pulls the porter toward the waki spot.)

Priest	*(continues to pray and sneaks up to the crab)* Look! Look! It's headed over there!
Porter	Ow! The closer you get, the harder he pinches! Ouch! Ouch!
Priest	You'll be free in no time now. Boron, boron, boron, boron.

(The crab reaches out for the priest's left ear and grabs it.)

Oww! Ouch! Ouch!

(The crab drags them both back and forth by their ears.)

Porter	Now what's wrong?
Priest	It's got me too!
Porter	Oh no!
Priest	Ouch! Ouch!
Porter	Ouch! Ouch! He keeps pinching harder! Oh! Ouch! Ouch!
Priest	What'll we do?
Porter	I can't bear it!

(The crab suddenly thrusts them both aside and exits.)

Priest	*(chases after the crab)* Where'd it go?
Porter	That way!
Priest	Quick! After it!

Porter   Please! Leave it alone!

Priest   Ahhh! I'm so mad! Catch it! Catch it!

Porter   Forget it! Leave it be!

Priest   Catch it! Catch it! Hey, you! You won't get away with
                this! You won't get away with this![11]

The Lunchbox Thief

THE LUNCHBOX THIEF[1]

Characters

Shite: Mountain Priest. Dressed in standard costume but without the travel chest.[2]

Ado: Woodcutter. Dressed in a striped robe and jacket with a belt; short kyōgen hakama bound to the knees; black leggings; a hood worn in the mountains; a fan. Over his right shoulder, he carries a scythe and a lunchbox attached to a pole. The scythe is wrapped in a length of white cotton cloth . The lunchbox is wrapped in straw, and tied with dark blue twine and has a pair of chopsticks attached.

Ado: Lunchbox Thief. Dressed in vest and matching short hakama.[3]

Woodcutter (*Enters and introduces himself at the shite spot.*)[4]

I live around here and I always go to the mountains for wood. Today, I'm going deep into the mountains to get kindling. (*circles the stage*) You know, there's no one with such back-breaking work as mine. Day in, day out, without any break,I set off with the morning dew and come home with the stars. It's a hard life. (*stops in front of the musicians spot*) Here I am at the foot of the mountain already. Once I start up, there'll be no place to rest. I left so early this morning that I'm very sleepy. I'll just take a short nap here.

(*Lies down facing the waki spot with his pole beside him.*)

Ahh....I'll stretch out here for a bit, have a bite to eat, and then climb the mountain.

Mountain Priest (*Enters and introduces himself at the shite spot.*)

I'm a mountain priest from Mount Haguro in Dewa. I've just done death-defying rites on Ōmine and Kazuragi and

I'm on my way home. But, what's the rush? I'll just take my time.

(*Circles the stage and stops at the first pine on the bridgeway.*)

What with our death-defying training, I tell you, I have attained marvelous powers! I can even pray a bird out of the sky. There's nothing that I can't do. And this time the retreat lasted so long that I'm really lucky to be going home at all. (*looks to the right*) So! Here I am already. From here on it's all uphill. But it's been a long trip and I'm done in. I just can't face that peak yet. Maybe I'll take a nap here.

(*Lies down in front of musicians spot, facing stagefront. He rests his head on his right arm with his prayer beads in his left hand.*)

Ahh! That feels good! I'll stretch out and take a nap.

Thief   (*Enters and introduces himself at the first pine on the bridgeway.*)

I live around here but I have an errand in one of the mountain villages about four or five miles from here. I'd better get a move on. (*begins to circle the stage*) It's certainly true that if you don't start, you'll never get to where you're going. But what with this and that, I've kept putting it off from one day to the next. (*notices the woodcutter at the waki spot*) What's this? Someone's asleep here! Aha! It looks like a woodcutter.(*notices the mountain priest*) Ha! There's a mountain priest asleep over here too.

(*Looks them both over.*)

Hmm... they're both out cold. Well! That looks to me like a lunchbox. I'll bet it's got the fixings for a meal. What luck! I left home so early I didn't have time to eat and now I'm really hungry. I've got a long way to go yet. I ought to be able to figure something out.

(Tiptoes between the mountain priest and woodcutter, and grabs the lunchbox. He kneels on one knee at the shite spot, and loosening the string around the box, he pulls out the chopsticks and begins to eat.)

Just as I thought! A meal! It looks delicious. Mmm! There's so much here. I can fill up on this all right.

(Startled by the woodcutter turning over in his sleep, he laughs.)[5]

That was close! Now I'd better finish this off. *(gobbles up the lunch)* Ohh! That was tasty! What a good dinner!

(Notices that the woodcutter is stirring and immediately thrusts the lunchbox over by the mountain priest and feigns sleep at upstage left.)[6]

Woodcutter   *(stands)* That's better! Just what I needed! A good, long nap. Now then, I'll have my lunch and be off. Hey! Where's my lunch? I don't understand it. When I left this morning I remember tying my lunch up, specially, with my scythe. Here's my scythe but where's my lunch gone to? This is very suspicious. *(spots the thief)* Aha! There's someone asleep over there. I'm going to wake him up and find out what's going on.

(Approaches the thief and rocks him until he wakes up. He then goes downstage and waits.)

Hey! Hey there! Hey, you! Wake up!

Thief   *(Feigns waking from a deep sleep and pretends not to be aware of the woodcutter.)*

Ahh! That was refreshing. Very refreshing. Such a peaceful nap.

Woodcutter   Hey you!

Thief   D'you mean me?

Woodcutter   Did you take my lunch?

Thief   Huh?

Woodcutter   I had my lunch right here, all wrapped up. I'm
                    asking you if you ate it!

Thief   What! I'm insulted. I happen to be from around here. I
                    was on an errand to the other side of the mountain when I
                    got tired and lay down for a nap. How would I know
                    what you've brought with you?

Woodcutter   But you've been sleeping right on the spot so don't try to
                    tell me you know nothing about it. Did you eat it or not?
                    C'mon, tell me!

Thief   Don't be stupid. I may look ragged but that doesn't make
                    me a lunch thief!

Woodcutter   You can talk all you like but no one's passed this way
                    except for you, so you look pretty guilty to me!

Thief   Well! What kind of justice is that? If you're going to be
                    that way, then what about that mountain priest asleep
                    over there? Doesn't he count?

Woodcutter   Yes, there is a mountain priest asleep over there, but who
                    ever heard of a mountain priest stealing a man's lunch?

Thief   C'mon! You don't know that. Look at him. That looks
                    a lot like a lunchbox next to his head.

Woodcutter   Hmm...(*approaches the mountain priest and peers at the
                    lunchbox*) Why, this is my lunch box! (*picks up the
                    lunchbox, angrily*) It's all gone! What a lousy thing to
                    do!

Thief   Better question him well!

                    (*Goes downstage and waits.*)

Woodcutter   (*Circles behind the mountain priest and prods him with his foot)*

Hey you! Hey!

Mountain Priest   Huh? (*picks up his prayer beads and stands*)

Woodcutter   What'd you mean, "huh?" You're no mountain priest! After I went to all that trouble to prepare a lunch you go and steal it from me! Isn't that right?

Mountain Priest   (*goes upstage*) What on earth are you talking about?

Woodcutter   (*at center stage*) You ate my lunch, didn't you!

Mountain Priest   What? I ate your lunch?

Woodcutter   That's right!

Mountain Priest   How insulting! Would a mountain priest steal a man's lunch?

Woodcutter   I don't care what you say. If it wasn't you then who was it? What happened to my lunch? Out with it!

Mountain Priest   You still don't believe me? Would a mountain priest lie? (*notices the thief*) Anyway, there's someone over there! Ask him!

Woodcutter   No, no! There's no need for that. It was you and nobody else! Quick! Let's have the truth!

Thief   Oh, reverend mountain priest, sir! There's the proof. Right there, where you were sleeping.

Mountain priest   The nerve! Who are you to pester a mountain priest?

Thief   I'm not pestering anybody. I was just passing by on an errand and decided to take a rest here.This woodcutter woke me up and said his lunch was missing. When I got up and looked around, I noticed that lunchbox beside you. So you can't get out of it. Now, tell us the truth!

Woodcutter	Yes! Here's the proof. Now then, come clean.
Mountain Priest	Well, well! So you were napping here too?
Thief	That's right.
Mountain Priest	Then, anyone of us could be guilty. There are three of us here. The woodcutter could have eaten it himself and then falsely accused us. Or, you could have stolen his lunch. Or, of course, you two might be suspicious of me as well. This is what my years of training have been for. I'll pray once and you'll have your lunch thief.
Woodcutter	Why, that's amazing! And will there be some proof if you pray?
Mountain Priest	Oh, yes! With one prayer I'll freeze the culprit's legs so he can't sit or stand.
Woodcutter	Then hurry! Pray!
Thief	(*laughs*) What a joke! A mountain priest calls out spirits, not lunchbox thieves!
Mountain Priest	Go ahead and laugh but I'm going to pray, and then you'll be sorry.
Thief	Sorry for what?
Mountain Priest	You'll be sorry, man!

incantation (noh style, dynamic mode)

> My months and years of training
> were for performing just such a miracle.[7]
> May the Guardian King lasso you in his rope.[8]
> I have strung up these irataka beads
> and when I rub them, "clackety, clack,"
> I offer a prayer.
> Boron, boron, boron, boron.

Thief	(*When the mountain priest begins to pray, he heads for the bridgeway.*)
	I'm not standing still for this. This is too wierd. I'll just ignore him and beat it out of here.
Woodcutter	Oh no you don't! You're not going anywhere!
Thief	Hey! What're you up to? What're you doing?
Woodcutter	Why, it's a miracle!
Thief	(*unable to move*) Ohh, help! Please! Stop![9]
Mountain priest	Irises under the bridge. Who planted the irises? It is I who planted irises. Boron, boron, boron, boron.[10]
Thief	I feel awful. Please let me go now!
Mountain priest	All right but let's hear the real story then.[11]
Thief	But it wasn't me, I tell you.
Mountain Priest	Didn't I tell you that if you don't fess up, I'll pray you dead?
Woodcutter	C'mon! We already know, so come clean!
Thief	But it wasn't me.
Mountain priest	Again, I rub my beads, Boron, boron, boron, boron. . .
Thief	(*wobbles about and falls backward on his seat*) Oh, help! Ouch! It hurts![12]
Woodcutter	Well! That was wonderful! I guess I spoke too soon. He's the thief all right. Now, leave him be, please.

Mountain Priest   That rascal? I'm going to pray him dead!

Woodcutter   Now, now. That's a terrible thing to say. Leave him alone. Come back home with me and relax instead.

Mountain Priest   No, no! I can't do that. I've got to finish him off.

Woodcutter   But I'm begging you. Please leave him alone.

Mountain priest   That's very generous of you.

Woodcutter   Leave him alone, all right?

Mountain priest   All right, then, I'll release him.

Woodcutter   No, don't release him. Just come home with me.

Mountain priest   I'll pray him dead for you here and now!

Woodcutter   Just forget about him and come with me. C'mon.

Mountain priest   Wait a minute.

Woodcutter   We don't have time. Just forget about him.

Thief   (*alone on stage*) Oh, it hurts; it hurts! Sir, sir! You're right! It was me. Please, help me! Help! Sir, sir! Oh, reverend mountain priest, sir! Please let me go! I can't stand this. I've confessed. Oh, I know I've done wrong. I know. You should never rob a man of his lunch. I can't feel my hands or feet! (*falls on his seat*) That's better. (*stands and exits*)[13]

Mushrooms

MUSHROOMS[1]

Characters

Shite: Mountain Priest. Dressed in a brocade robe with geometric designs; kyōgen hakama bound to the knees; a three-quarter length travel cloak with broad sleeves in silk or gauze; a black, pleated cap; a mantle studded with tufted white or orange cotton balls; a small sword; a fan; prayer beads.

Ado: Neighbor. Dressed in long hakama with a matching vest.

Ado: The mushrooms. Dressed in a variety of hats and masks. With the exception of the "princess mushroom," all the mushrooms are male and are dressed in hakama bound to the knees. The princess mushroom wears a silk kimono, a draping belt, and a red scarf wrapped around her head.[2] Matsutake wears a pointed bamboo hat and mask. Shiitake wears a black laquered coolie hat and mask. Thanksgiving mushroom (*reishi*)[3] wears a brown wicker coolie hat and mask. Princess mushroom wears a sedge coolie hat and an *oto* mask (comical, round faced young girl mask). Demon mushroom wears a demon cap (a black cloth cap which comes to a tufted point at the top), a sedge or cypress coolie hat, an umbrella, and the fierce Buaku mask.[4]

(The matsutake mushroom enters and plants himself, crouching, at center stage.)[5]

Neighbor   I live in the neighborhood. For some reason this year, for the first time ever, mushrooms have popped up in my garden. No matter how many times I pull them out by the next morning they're right back where they were. I've never seen anything like it. There's a powerful mountain priest not far from here. I think I'll ask him to cast a spell for me and see if that gets rid of them. It's a puzzle all right. But if he'd just cast a spell then we'd know what was going on.

(Circles the stage and stops at the shite spot.)

111

Ah! I've only just left home and here I am already. I'll announce myself.

(Goes to the first pine and drops to one knee, facing the curtain.)

Priest

(Enters, lifting his legs high as if mountain climbing and marches down the bridgeway while reciting in the dynamic mode.)[6]

Before the window of the nine realms of the senses,
on a pallet of the ten vehicles of the law,
sprinkled with the holy waters of yoga,
(changes to spoken style)
cleansed by the moon of the three mysteries,[7]
who goes there?

Neighbor

(leaps forward, lunging at the priest) It's me.

Priest

(falls on his seat) Hey you! I didn't know who it was, flying up in my face like that. What d'you want?

Neighbor

It's just that, for some reason, this year for the first time, these mushrooms have been popping up in my garden. No matter how many times I pull them out, by the next morning they're right back where they were I've tried everything and I still can't get rid of them. It's really weird. I'd be very grateful if you'd come and cast a spell.

Priest

Well, well, so that's the trouble? I've never heard of anything like it before. Of course mushrooms do spring up but it's odd that they should keep coming back after you pull them out.

Neighbor

Exactly. That's why I felt that it was out of the ordinary and so, naturally, I came to you.

Priest

Well, I'm engaged in some special rites at the moment, so I really shouldn't go anywhere. But, for you, I'll do it.

Neighbor	Now that's nice of you. Could you come right away?
Priest	Of course, let's go.
Neighbor	After you, sir.
Priest	You go first and lead the way.
Neighbor	Shall I then?
Priest	Yes, yes, go on.
Neighbor	In that case, I'll lead the way. Please follow me.
Priest	Of course.

(The neighbor goes first and circles the stage, stopping at the shite pillar. The mountain priest follows, passing the neighbor at the shite pillar and stopping at the first pine on the bridgeway.)

Neighbor	*(circles the stage)* I'm so glad you could come right away today.
Priest	*(follows the neighbor)* As I told you, I shouldn't go out at all, but for you, I've made this exception.
Neighbor	I really appreciate it. Here we are already.
Priest	This is the place then?
Neighbor	Please go ahead.

(They exchange places. The priest goes to the shite pillar while the neighbor goes to the first pine on the bridgeway. They turn and face one another.)

Priest	Now, where is this mushroom?
Neighbor	There it is. *(points to the mushroom crouched at center*

stage rear)

Priest	Wow! Is that it?
Neighbor	Yes, sir.
Priest	Well! I've seen mushrooms in my day but never one that big before!
Neighbor	It's really creepy.
Priest	Not at all. There's nothing creepy about it. This is a matsutake mushroom.
Neighbor	Excuse me, sir. You say this is a matsutake mushroom?
Priest	That's right.
Neighbor	If you say so. It seems awfully big for a matsutake.
Priest	So, you've never had this happen before?
Neighbor	Oh no. I've never even heard of anything like it before. I know it looks bad; that's why I'm so uneasy.
Priest	Nothing to worry about. I'll get rid of it with one spell.
Neighbor	Thank you , sir.

incantation (noh style, dynamic mode)

Priest	(*Chants.*) A tokin is a foot-long piece of cloth dyed black, folded in pleats and popped on the bean, therefore it's called a tokin.[8]
Neighbor	Ah ha.
Priest	(*Resumes chanting.*)

Irataka prayer beads, these are not;[9]
(*examines the beads*)
I strung together any old beads and called them irataka.
If I offer a prayer
(*begins to rub beads and sing in noh style*)
how can a miracle fail to occur?
Boron, boron, boron, boron.

(*Stops rubbing the beads and turns on the mushroom which faces forward and begins to quiver.*)

Neighbor	Excuse me, sir. It's moving!
Priest	A miracle!
Neighbor	Yes, sir!
Priest	(*faces the mushroom*) Boron, boron.
Neighbor	(*watches as a second mushroom shuffles in from the little door at upstage left*) Oh no! Oh sir! Sir!
Priest	Well, what is it?
Neighbor	(*points*) Another big one's sprung up over there!
Priest	You're right! It looks like a shiitake mushroom.
Neighbor	Quick! Pray it away!
Priest	Yes, of course. I'll show you how it's done.
Neighbor	Please!

incantation (noh style)

Priest   Under the bridge the irises bloom.
Who planted the irises?
Who planted the irises?[10]

(*Two more mushrooms pop through the little door*

upstage left)

Neighbor	Oh sir! Sir!
Priest	What? What is it?
Neighbor	Look at that! They're springing up everywhere!
Priest	What? More have come up? Oh! This one's a Thanksgiving mushroom.
Neighbor	Really? A Thanksgiving mushroom?
Priest	Yes, we ought to celebrate!
Neighbor	Well, whatever it is, they're multiplying!
Priest	Of course, that's to be expected. Didn't you say that you pulled them up again and again but they kept coming back? With my extraordinary powers, I'll make them all pop up. There are already so many here that I doubt there could be anymore. Since I've prayed them all up, I'll now pray them away. You ought to have more faith.
Neighbor	All right, sir.

incantation (noh style)

Priest   I will pray that the fierce Guardian King[11]
lassoes them in his holy rope.
How can a miracle fail to occur?
Boron, boron, boron, boron.

(*As he prays, two or three more hop out from the little door upstage left.*)

Neighbor	Excuse me, sir! Another whole crowd has popped up!
Priest	Look at that! A bunch of them have sprung up! This must be a princess mushroom!

(*Wanders about, examining them as they shuffle about the stage.*)

What a sight! (*looks concerned*)

Neighbor   Uh...sir?

Priest   Huh?

Neighbor   What's going on here anyway?

Priest   (*looks hopeless*) Nothing to worry about. Things always increase before they disappear. Relax.

Neighbor   (*trembles*) Well, I don't know about that. Just get rid of them.

Priest   You're right.

(*Prays alternately at one mushroom and then another. The demon mushroom, who has entered silently onto the bridgeway, crouches behind the first pine. The priest keeps on praying without noticing him.*)

Neighbor   (*startled by the demon mushroom*) Sir, sir!

Priest   (*ignores him*) Boron, boron.

Neighbor   (*louder*) Wait a moment, sir!

Priest   Well, what now?

Neighbor   Forget about those. Will you take a look at this one! You prayed up a really big one this time!

Priest   (*Catches sight of the demon mushroom and is discouraged but still tries to keep up a good front.*)

Oh! Well! This is truly miraculous. That must be a giant demon mushroom. It hasn't opened yet but when it does, it'll really be something to see.

Neighbor	They keep multiplying. It's driving me crazy. Until now I've always thought of you as a living Fudō. I believed you could solve any problem. But today, when I call on you, your prayers are useless. My entire garden is filled with mushrooms. If I'd never summoned you, things wouldn't be this bad!
Priest	What?! That's simply nonsense. Why, with my great powers, I can pray the ocean dry. I can pray a mountain to the ground. But these mushrooms now... hmmm... clearing them out is really going to be hard. I wonder what to do?
Neighbor	It's that stupidity of yours that has gotten us into this. I don't care how you do it, just pray them away. Quick!
Priest	Humph. Fool! As if babbling away like that is of any help. *(speaks in a determined manner)* All right, I'll make the sign of the eggplant this time.[12] In one swoop I'll wipe out all of these mushrooms.
Neighbor	Do as you like. Just get on with it.
Priest	*(Faces front and makes an eggplant sign. Then, he claps his hands suddenly and the mushrooms begin to quiver. Only the demon mushroom remains as it was.)*
	A miracle!
Neighbor	Hurry up! Pray, pray!
	(The mushrooms quiver. Repulsed by the sight of them, the mountain priest faces front and prays, but is unable to resist glancing back at the mushrooms.)

incantation (noh style)

Priest	No matter how many mushrooms there may be, when I make the sign of the eggplant and offer a prayer,

how can they fail to disappear?
Boron, boron. . .

*(Glances around at the mushrooms. Most of them move
in to surround the neighbor; one or two head for the
mountain priest.)*

Neighbor   *(surrounded and scared)* What should I do?

*(Tries to avoid them but they come even closer. The ones
that were around the mountain priest come too.)*

Sir, sir! The mushrooms are all over me!

Priest   Stand perfectly still.

*(Chants intently, turning in one direction and then
another.)*

Boron, boron, boron, boron.

*(The mushrooms become more tenacious in their pursuit
of the frightened neighbor.)*

Neighbor   Hurry! Pray them away! Please!

*(Flees to the bridgeway with the mushrooms quivering
around him. At the first pine, he finally extricates
himself.)*

Help! I'm scared! I'm scared!

*(Flees down the bridgeway with the mushrooms in hot
pursuit.)*

Priest   *(Faces the fleeing neighbor and tries to stop him by
praying.)*

Stand perfectly still!

(Follows the neighbor to the shite spot and gazes

after him as he exits pursued by mushrooms.) Hey, hey! What's this? Hey, hey! This won't do. He's gone already. Now I am in a fix. I'm all on my own. At least I've gotten rid of most of the mushrooms. (*spots the demon mushroom*) What's that great demon mushroom doing here still? (*faces front*) Oh well, maybe I'd better get out of here too.

(*Glances fearfully behind him and tries to slip past the demon mushroom along the bridgeway. The demon suddenly opens his umbrella, blocking the way. Surprised, the priest retreats to the main stage looking alarmed and repulsed. He peeks at the mushroom from behind the shite pillar.*)

It's moving! I can't take any more of this. I'll make the eggplant sign again and get rid of it.

(*Turns to the mushroom and makes the eggplant sign, then claps his hands.*)

incantation (noh style)

Priest   No matter how evil a demon mushroom you are,
                   when a mountain priest, the living body of the Buddha,
                   makes the sign of the eggplant and prays,
                   how can a miracle fail to occur?
                   Boron, boron, boron, boron.

(*During the prayer, the mushroom enters the stage and they meet face to face.*)

I make the sign of the eggplant.
Boron, boron, boron. . .

(*Continues to pray, backing up as he does so. When he reaches the bridgeway, the mushroom tries to close the umbrella over the priest's head. The priest falls backward on his seat.*)

I make the sign of the eggplant,

the sign of the eggplant.

(*Rises as he prays. The mushroom again attempts to catch him in the umbrella.*)

Help! Nothing works! Help! Help!

(*Runs down the bridgeway and exits with the mushroom in pursuit.*)[13]

Owls

OWLS[1]

Characters

    Shite: Mountain Priest. Dressed in the usual mountain priest costume, but with broad stiff white hakama, a three-quarter length travel cloak worn over a yellow checked robe and a hood with a pointed top. [2]

    Ado: Older brother. Dressed in a vest with matching long hakama or a vest with ankle-length hakama.

    Ado: Tarō. Dressed in a soft white silk under-kimono, long hakama. His hair is loose and wild and he wears a strip of red cloth bound around his forehead and draped on one side.[3]

Brother   (*enters and announces himself at the shite spot*) I live in the neighborhood. I don't know what's going on but ever since my little brother returned from the mountains he's been possessed by something or other. I've tried all sorts of cures but nothing works. There's a powerful mountain priest nearby so I've decided to ask him to perform a spell for me. (*circles stage*) I just don't understand it! How on earth could he have gotten into such bad shape? Oh well, if I can get that mountain priest to come and pray, he should be back to his old self in no time. (*stops at the shite spot*) Here I am already. I'll just announce myself.

(*Proceeds to the first pine on the bridgeway and kneels on one knee facing the curtain.*)

Priest   (*Enters, marching with legs high as if climbing a mountain, and chanting in noh style.*)

Before the window of the nine realms of the senses;
On a pallet of the ten vehicles of the law;
Sprinkled with the holy waters of yoga;
(*changes to spoken style*)
Purified by the moon of the three mysteries;
Who goes there![4]

Brother	(*leaps up as if to charge him*) It's me!
Priest	(*falls on his seat in surprise and slowly rises*) What? It's you, is it?
Brother	Yes, sir.
Priest	Hey! I didn't know who it was—flying up in my face like that—what do you want?
Brother	It's just that, well, you remember my little brother?
Priest	Of course, of course. I know Tarō. What's the matter with him?
Brother	That's just it. He came down from Mount Obi and he's been possessed by something ever since. Could you come and perform a spell? I'd be grateful to you, sir.
Priest	Hold on! That's a bit difficult. (*sings in noh style*) I'm in the midst of some special rites and shouldn't go anywhere. (*returns to normal speech*) But, for you, I'll do it.[5]
Brother	Thank you, sir. Can you come right away?
Priest	Of course. Let's go!
Brother	Well then, after you, sir.
Priest	You go first and lead the way.
Brother	Shall I go first, sir?
Priest	Yes, yes. Go ahead.
Brother	Then, I'll lead the way. Please, follow me. (*leads the way as they circle the stage*)
Priest	Of course. (*follows the brother*)

Brother	I'm so glad you could come as soon as I asked.
Priest	Don't bother to thank me. With one prayer I'll have him back to normal.
Brother	Thank you, sir.
Priest	Tarō is usually so healthy. It's hard to know what to make of this.
Brother	(*stops at the shite spot*) Here we are already.
Priest	(*passes the brother and stops at the first pine on the bridgeway*) This is the place then?
Brother	Please come in. (*they exchange places*)
Priest	All right. (*in noh style*) Now, where is the sick boy?
Brother	I made him lie down in the back. I'll go and get him.
Priest	Hurry. Bring him out.
Brother	Certainly, sir.
	(*Goes offstage and returns with Taro leaning against him with one arm over his shoulder. He supports Tarō around the waist and holds on to his right hand.*)
	Tarō! Tarō! The master is here. Try to pull yourself together! Excuse me, sir. Here's Tarō!
Priest	What? This is Tarō? (*peers quizzically into Tarō's face*)[6]
Brother	Yes, sir.
Priest	Oh, no. How pitiful. He's in a bad way.
Brother	Exactly, sir.

Priest   All right, let me examine him.

                      (*Approaches gingerly with his beads dangling from his
                      left hand, and leans forward.*)

Brother   Please help him, sir.

                      (*Watches as the priest stretches out his hand and rubs
                      Tarō's head vigorously.*)

                      What're you doing? What're you doing to him?

Priest   (*Backs off as if frightened and switches his beads to his
                      right hand.*)

                      Take it easy. Usually you take a pulse from the right or
                      left wrist but in cases of possession, you take it from the
                      head. It's known as the head pulse.

Brother   I see. How is he?

Priest   Very bad. Very bad. It's really evil all right.

Brother   It's evil, is it?

Priest   (*Peers up at Tarō's face and can't seem to suppress his
                      amusement at it.*)

                      Probably a high fever. Taro! Hey there, Tarō! He seems
                      to be in a daze.

Brother   He's lost conciousness completely.

Priest   Just as I thought.

Brother   Could you say a spell, sir? We'd be really grateful.

Priest   That's easy. I'll pray once and have him back to normal.

Brother   Thank you, sir.

incantation (noh style, dynamic mode)

Priest

(*Faces front and performs a hiraki, then walks toward the waki spot and begins to chant.*)

The ascetic will now offer an incantation.
I follow in the path of the Great Ascetic En.
I have climbed the twin peaks of Ōmine and Kazuragi
and entered the gates of the Diamond Mandala
and the Womb Mandala.
I wear the *suzukake* mantle
Brushing aside the mountain mists of the seven treasures,
I am shielded by a mantle of fortitude
from the filth of this world.
These beads (*examines his prayer beads*)
are not irataka,
they're just any old beads I've strung up
and call "irataka." (*winds them up in his hands*)
If I offer a prayer (*rubs the beads*)
how can a miracle fail to occur?[7]
Boron, boron, boron, boron. . . (*faces Tarō, who begins to tremble*)

Brother

Hold on! He's in pain!

Priest

Another minute and he'll be cured.

Brother

That's fine, then.

Priest

(*prays hard*) Boron, boron, boron, boron.

Tarō

(*Writhes in pain and flings himself about until he faces the priest and hoots.*)

Whooo!

Priest

(*startled, he stops praying*) Ha! I don't know what it was but he said something all right! (*frees his left hand from the beads and takes them up in his right*)

Brother	Yes, he did say something, sir.
Priest	He sounds bewitched to me. What did he say?
Brother	It sounded like "whooo."
Priest	Exactly! But that doesn't make any sense. Can you understand it?
Brother	No, except that he said something about knocking down an owl's nest when he was in the mountains.
Priest	So that's it! Say no more. It's a case of owl possession. It's a very persistent owl, but don't worry. I'll make the sign of the crow[8] and have him free in no time. Now then, I'll pray out the owl.
Brother	Thank you, sir.

incantation (noh style, dynamic mode)

Priest	No matter how frightening an owl spirit
	When I make the sign of the crow
	and offer a prayer
	how can you refuse to go?
	Boron, boron, boron, boron.[9]
	Oh no! This is terrible! Now the older brother is possessed too. What a persistent owl. Oh no! They're both in pain.
Brother	(*Begins to yawn as he watches Tarō and then stretches his arms and legs, turns to the priest, and hoots.*)
	Whooo.
Priest	(*Alarmed and disgusted he stops praying and studies both of them.*)
	Ugh! That's disgusting! Get away!
Tarō	(*hoots in pain*) Whoo!

Brother   (*hoots in pain*) Whooo!

Priest   (*Tries to sneak away but as he heads up the bridgeway
               the brothers hoot again and again. He returns to the
               waki spot.*)

               This is terrible. I can't just leave them like this. What'll
               I do? Oh, what's there to be scared of, anyway? I'll just
               give a short prayer and free them both instantly. (*takes a
               deep breath and begins to pray*)

incantation (noh style, dynamic mode)

               Oh persistent owl!
               Flapping about possessing people here and there.
               If I offer a prayer
               How can you fail to disappear?
               Boron, boron, boron, boron. . .

               (*Begins to yawn and look ill. He faces Tarō and makes
               the sign of the crow.*)

               Boron, boron, boron, boron. . .

               (*The brothers continue to hoot in pain.*)

               Boron, boron, boron, boron. . .

               (*Begins to get sleepy and wavers about. His "boron,
               boron," changes into "whoo, whoo."*)

               Whoo, whooo, whooo, whooo.

               (*Tarō and his brother dart about the stage, hooting. The
               three stagger and get tangled up together. The brother
               staggers off stage followed by the priest and finally,
               Tarō.*)[10]

柿山伏

Persimmons

PERSIMMONS[1]

Characters

Shite: Mountain Priest. Dressed in a brocade robe with
geometric designs; kyōgen hakama bound to the knees; a
three-quarter length travel cloak with broad sleeves in
silk or gauze; a black, pleated cap; a mantle studded with
tufted white or orange cotton balls; a small sword; prayer
beads.

Ado: Orchard Owner. Dressed in long or ankle-length hakama
with a matching vest.

(*Entrance music*: noh flute, small shoulder drum, large hip drum.)[2]

Priest   (*Marches down the bridgeway lifting his legs high as if
mountain climbing and stops at the shite spot. He faces
the musicians spot and sings in noh style.*)

shidai (noh style)

A mountain priest with no conch shell to toot,
A mountain priest with no conch shell to toot,
blows lies along his route.[3]

(*faces front and introduces himself*)

I'm a mountain priest from Mount Haguro in Dewa. I've
just done death-defying rites on Ōmine and Kazuragi and
now I'm going home. But what's the rush? I'll just stroll
along.

(*Begins to circle the stage.*)

You know, we undergo such terrible, death-defying rites
that I've gotten great powers. I can do anything. Why, in
an instant I could pray a bird right out of the sky. This
trip's been especially long so I feel lucky just to be going
home in one piece.

135

(*Arrives back at the shite spot.*)

Oh dear! I haven't eaten since morning. My stomach's
really empty! But as the saying goes, "if you haven't a
home, you can't demand food." That's a bitter truth all
right.

(*Turns toward the waki position.*)

What'll I do? Hah! There's a persimmon tree. (*looks
around*) Hmm....every tree around here is a persimmon.
Well, well! Persimmons everywhere!

(*Looks toward the waki spot.*)

This one's got the most fruit. It's a beauty. What luck!
But I wonder where the owner is? I'd like to ask him for
one of those persimmons.

(*Goes to stage center and looks down the bridgeway.*)

Hello? Hello? Anybody there? I'd like to pick a
persimmon from your tree. Is the owner about? Oh dear!
He doesn't seem to be around.

(*Glances at the waki spot.*)

Now what'll I do? I know! Of course it's wrong, but he
won't mind. First, I'll toss a pebble and try to knock one
down.

(*Tucks his prayer beads into his breast and kneels on one
knee. Making a sweeping movement over the stage floor
with one hand, he searches for a stone and then stands.*)

One, two, three! (*hurls with his right hand*) There she
goes! There she goes! It didn't even reach. I'll try
again.

(*Searches with his right hand as before.*)[4]

One, two, three! There she goes! There she goes! Not even close. I ought to be able to think of something.

(*Looks toward the waki spot.*)

I know! They're so ripe that if I shake the tree they're bound to fall. I'll give it a good shake.

(*Wraps both arms around the waki pillar and shakes hard.*)

One, two, three!

(*Laughs and returns to center stage.*)

It's too big for me all by myself. Too bad. I'm so hungry. I wonder what to do.

(*Looks toward the waki spot.*)

Hmm . . . those branches would be perfect for climbing. I'll give it a try.

(*Approaches the chorus spot and stops there. He drops to one knee and removes his small sword which he places on the stage. He then stands and approaches the waki spot where he climbs the railing by the waki pillar or simply stands beside it.*)

Now, if I'm going to eat the persimmons, I'd better cast a spell to multiply the fruit. Then it'll all be to the owner's advantage. One, two, three! Up I go! Up I go! Ah ha! Wonderful! I shinnied right up! No problem at all.

(*Stands on the railing and looks about. He comments on the fruit and then begins to eat.*)[5]

Ha, ha! This is splendid! It looks quite different from up here. It's even better than from below. Now then, I'll just try one. Oh boy! This is delicious! I'll try another.

Oooh! It's so sweet! Here's a really juicy, ripe one. The juicier, the better! (*sucks on the fruit*) Mmm, this is sweet. It's like eating sugar.

Owner   (*Stands at the first pine on the bridgeway and, facing the audience, introduces himself.*)

I'm from these parts. It's been several days since I've checked my persimmon crop. The fruit should be ripe about now. I think I'll go and have a look.

(*Enters the stage proper and circles, stopping at the shite spot.*)

Really, there's no business like trees. You never lift a finger and still they blossom and bear fruit. Oh! I'm here already. Now, I'll see how my persimmons are coming along.

(*Looks about and proceeds to center stage and from there to the waki spot.*)

I haven't been here for a while and now most of the fruit is ripe. Well, well, they look splendid. I guess I'll be having quite a crop this year.

(*At about this point, the mountain priest casually spits out a pit which hits the owner in the head.*)

Who's there!

(*Raises his right hand to his head and then picks up the pit.*)

Someone threw this! What's going on here?

(*Struck by a second pit.*)

Again! All right! What's the meaning of this? There doesn't seem to be anyone around.

(*Looks around and spots the priest in the tree.*)

Huh? Something's up in the tree! (*recognizes that it's a priest*)[6] Isn't that the limit! I wondered what it was and it turns out to be a mountain priest snitching my persimmons. Well, well! The rascal! What'll I do? Hmm. Ha! I have it! He's no ordinary thief so I'll have a little fun with him.

(*Coughs and, coming forward, gazes up at the waki pillar.*)

Hello! There's something stuck up in my persimmon tree.

Priest	Bless the three treasures! I'm caught! (*surprised, he crouches down suddenly*)
Owner	Well, well! It's got a black head. Of course! It's a crow!
Priest	Thank heaven! He thinks I'm a crow.
Owner	Dear me! That crow is after my persimmons. But if it's really a crow, it'll caw.
Priest	He wants me to caw.
Owner	Isn't it going to caw?
Priest	What'll I do?
Owner	Either caw or I'll cut you in ribbons. Well, are you going to caw?
Priest	I've got to caw.
Owner	That's it! That's the way! It looks like he's going to caw!
Priest	(*faces the owner and caws*) Kokaa. Kokaa.

Owner	Kokaa, kokaa. (*bursts into laughter*) Beautiful! But, I seem to have been mistaken.
Priest	He says he was mistaken.
Owner	It's a dog!
Priest	This is terrible. He says I'm a dog!
Owner	How can a dog climb a tree? But there's no doubt about it, it's a dog, all right. A dog would try to frighten me away.
Priest	He says I've got to scare him off.
Owner	Are you going to bark?
Priest	What'll I do?
Owner	If you don't bark, I'll knock you down from there. Are you going to bark, or not?
Priest	I'd better bark.
Owner	Ho! He's about to bark!
Priest	(*faces the owner and barks*) Byo, byo, byo, byo.
Owner	Byo, byo! (*laughs*) Great barking! But I was wrong; it's not a dog, after all.
Priest	Not again! He says he was wrong.
Owner	It's a monkey!
Priest	Oh no! Now he says I'm a monkey.
Owner	Monkeys love persimmons so he's been after them. It's a monkey all right. But if it's a monkey, it'll scratch and screech.

Priest	He says I've got to scratch and screech.
Owner	Are you going to screech?
Priest	What'll I do?
Owner	If you don't screech, I'll skewer you on a stick! Well, are you going to screech?
Priest	I'd better screech.
Owner	Ho! Looks like he's about to screech!
Priest	(*scratches his bottom*) Kya, kya, kya, kya.
Owner	Kya, kya, kya! (*laughs*) Wonderful screeching!

(*He performs a hiraki at the shite spot.*)

This is really fun. I wonder if there's something he can't possibly do? Ah ha! I've got it! I know what I'll ask him to do. (*comes forward and turns to face the priest*) Too bad! I thought it was a monkey but I'm wrong again.

Priest	He says he was wrong again.
Owner	It's a hawk!
Priest	What! Now he says I'm a hawk! Of course, they do say that mountain priests can transform themselves into falcons but . . . do I look like a hawk, I wonder?
Owner	No doubt about it, it's a hawk. If you're a hawk, you'll spread your wings.
Priest	Oh! I know what I'll do.

(*Slides around to face the owner and takes out his fan. He opens the fan and, stretching out his arms, waves*

them up and down. He then grabs the pillar with his left hand and waves the fan up and down with the right.)
Hiii, yoro, yoro, yoro, yoro . . .

Owner   Well, well! He spread his wings. Any minute now he'll fly.

Priest   (*spreads out his arms*) What a nuisance. How can I possibly jump from way up here?

Owner   Aren't you going to fly?

Priest   What'll I do?

Owner   If you don't fly, I'll drag you down. Well, what about it? Are you going to fly or not?

Priest   I'd better fly.

Owner   Hey! He's going to take off! Hey! Hey! He's going to fly!

(*Removes his fan and begins to tap a rhythm on his left palm while hopping from foot to foot, gradually increasing the tempo.*)

He's going to fly. Up he goes! He's going to fly. Up he goes! He's going to fly. Up he goes! He's going to fly.

Priest   (*Flaps his arms in time to the owner's beat.*)

Hiiii, yoro, yoro, yoro.

(*As he cries out, he turns to face the owner and leaps, falling on his seat.*)

Owner   (*watches the fall*) It looked like he was going to make it but it was no go.

Priest   (*sits up, closes his fan and puts it away*) Hey, hey! You there!

Owner	What?
Priest	Scoundrel! You dare to compare me, a great mountain priest, to birds and beasts and even a hawk? I thought I must have turned myself into a falcon since we can do that, you know, when we're at the height of our powers. But then I tried to fly and it seems my wings hadn't grown in yet. Because of you I fell, splat. Now you'll have to take me home with you and bandage my bruises.
Owner	You've got to be kidding! What's the difference between a thief of a mountain priest like you and a monkey or a dog?
Priest	Better watch what you say. Are you going to help me?
Owner	It ought to be obvious. Why should I care about a thief? Let alone one that demands first aid!
Priest	(*Kneels on one knee and thrusts the other leg forward.*)
	Do you mean that? Because I'll show you a thing or two!
Owner	Who will?
Priest	I will!
Owner	(*laughs*) You! Ooh, watch me shake.
Priest	You're sure about this?
Owner	And what if I am?
Priest	You'll be sorry! (*stands*) You'll wish you'd done as I asked, man!
	(*faces front, removes his prayer beads and takes them in his right hand.*)

incantation (noh style, dynamic mode)

Parting the clouds at the peak,
piling up years of merit from austerities:
one meal a day, total fasting,
standing rites, seated rites.
This great mountain priest entreats
En the Ascetic and all of the gods and all of the Buddhas
to please come to my aide with all of your powers.[7]
I roll my tightly strung irataka beads,
"clackety, clack," in my hands and I offer up this prayer:
boron, boron, boron, boron. (*stops and faces the owner*)

Owner   What's all that mumbo jumbo? Whatever you're mumbling, it's all nonsense. (*heads for the bridgeway*)

Priest   Boron, boron, boron. (*prays owner to a stop*)

Owner   (*halts at the first pine on the bridgeway*) Hey! What're you doing to me?

incantation (noh style, dynamic mode)

Priest   Irises under the bridge.
Who planted the irises?
It is I who planted the irises.[8]
Boron, boron, boron, boron. . .

(*Advances to the shite spot and prays backing up.*)

Owner   What're you up to?

(*As if paralyzed, he staggers backward in time to the prayer, and falls slightly forward of front center stage.*)[9]

Oh! Oh! Help! Please! Forgive me! Oh, oh! Look, I've said I'm sorry so please let me go!

Priest   Let you go?

Owner   Yes, I'll do anything. Just let me go.

Priest	Now you see the powers of a great mountain priest. Take me home and bandage my bruises. Now!
Owner	I give up. I'll have to take care of him. All right. Hop on my back. (*kneels on one knee*)
Priest	That's more like it. Careful! (*tries to get up on the owner's back*)
Owner	(*grabs the mountain priest by the right wrist*) There! You fool!
Priest	What're you doing!
Owner	What am I doing? You've caused enough trouble.
Priest	What're you doing? Hey!
Owner	(*hurls him down*) This is how I treat rascals like you!
Priest	(*falling to the floor*) Oh! How could you!
Owner	(*laughs*) Beautiful! Oh sir! Sir! I'm so scared of you. I'm so scared!
Priest	Hey, hey! You there!
Owner	What?
Priest	You've been picking on me–me, a great mountain priest. Now, I'm going to pray you dead.
Owner	(*exits down the bridgeway*) Oooh! I'm scared! You think you can pray a man dead? You?
Priest	Someone! Catch him![10]

Sacroiliac

SACROILIAC[1]

Chararacters
    Shite: Mountain priest
    Ado: Grandfather
    Ado: Tarō Kaja

(Tarō Kaja enters and stands slightly downstage from the shite spot.)

shidai (noh style)

Priest
    (Enters the stage and stops at the shite spot. He sings facing the musicians spot.)

    On his way down from the three peaks
    On his way down from the three peaks
    A mountain priest is grand indeed.

    I'm a mountain priest. I've just been through sacred rites everywhere. I've been on Mount Ōmine for some time and I'm headed for home now. But I think I'll stop on my way and see my grandfather who lives around here. It's been ages since I've seen him. He's over one hundred years old, so I worry about him.

    (Circles stage and stops at shite spot.)

    After so many rites, I'm lucky just to be going home in one piece. Ha! Here I am already. You know, I've been gone for so long, I'd better announce myself. Hello! Is anybody there!

Tarō Kaja
    Who is it? Oh! I wondered who it could be. We haven't seen you for such a long time. You're looking splendid.

Priest
    Yes, indeed, it has been a long time. I'm glad to see you're looking pretty good yourself.

Tarō Kaja
    Thank you, sir.

Priest
    Now then, how is the old fellow? I've been worried

about him.

Tarō Kaja   No need to worry, sir. He's been just fine.

Priest   He's been well then?

Tarō Kaja   Yes, sir.

Priest   Good, good! What a relief! I'm delighted to hear it. I've been away so long, I was quite worried.

Tarō Kaja   That's to be expected, sir. Why, ever since you left, your grandfather has been worrying about you from morning to night.

Priest   That's only natural. I've missed him too. Let him know I'm here. I'd like to see him right away.

Tarō Kaja   Yes, sir. I know he'll be pleased. Do come in.

Priest   Of course.

(Goes downstage and faces front while Tarō Kaja follows as far as the shite spot.)

Tarō Kaja   *(turns to curtain on the bridgeway)* Hello? Hello! Grandfather! The young master has come!

Grandfather   *(Enters with a cane, grunting, and stops at the first pine.)*

Uh, uh, uh ...What's that you say? We're having fish for dinner? Well, well, that is good news! This old man's teeth are falling out so don't give me any bones.

Tarō Kaja   Yes, of course, sir. You'll have fish today, but what I wanted to tell you is that the young master has arrived.

Grandfather   What? What's that? The young master is here?

Tarō Kaja   Exactly, sir.

Grandfather	I don't believe it.
Tarō Kaja	It's true.
Grandfather	(*laughs*) My, my! How I've missed that boy. How I've missed that boy! Where is he?
Tarō Kaja	I asked him to come in.
Grandfather	(*proceeds to center stage*) Uh, uh, umph, umph, mmmm. It's been a long time. A very long time. Where's the young master?

(Stops at center stage and peers around. Tarō Kaja brings him the barrel seat.)

Priest	Here I am, sir!
Tarō Kaja	Your seat, sir. (*seats the grandfather at center stage*)
Grandfather	(*leans forward on his staff*) Go on with you now! Where are you?
Priest	Excuse me, grandfather. It's me!
Grandfather	Hmm! Over there are you? (*laughs*) It's good to see you, lad.
Priest	Thank you, sir. I know I haven't visited for a while but just hearing how well you've been does my heart good.
Grandfather	Yes, yes. Your grandfather is much the same. I'm happy to see you looking so fit yourself.
Priest	Thank you, sir. I couldn't be better.
Grandfather	Mmm... You've been away so long that ...Oh, Tarō Kaja!
Tarō Kaja	Yes, sir!

Grandfather	He's really grown, hasn't he?
Tarō Kaja	Indeed he has, sir.
Grandfather	Hmm, it's a real joy to see you. You've been gone so long I'd really like to give you a treat. Tarō Kaja! We don't have anything in the house, do we?
Tarō Kaja	Nothing much, sir.
Grandfather	Hmm ...If I'd known you were coming I'd have put something by. What can I give him? Ah ha! I know! That's just the ticket! Just the ticket! You always loved puppy dogs. The dog had a litter the other day. How would you like a pup?
Priest	You're very kind.
Grandfather	Tarō Kaja!
Tarō Kaja	Yes, sir!
Grandfather	Pick out the best of the speckled ones for him.
Tarō Kaja	Yes, sir.
Priest	Grandfather seems to think I'm still a child.
Tarō Kaja	He does, indeed, sir.
Grandfather	Hmmm ...
Priest	I've been away for so long that your back's gotten quite crippled.
Grandfather	What's he say?
Priest	I said, your back's gotten quite bent.
Grandfather	Oh ho! You're right there! Your grandfather gets older by the year. My eyes have gone, my ears are going, and

now my back is bent so badly that I can hardly say my
morning and evening prayers. I'm quite an invalid.

Priest Yes, I can see that. You know, I've just come from
Mount Ōmine where I did death-defying rites. I can even
pray a bird down from the sky. So why don't you let me
perform some spells to straighten up your back? This is
just what I've trained for.

Grandfather Tarō Kaja!

Tarō Kaja Yes, sir?

Grandfather What's he going on about now?

Tarō Kaja He says he'd like to perform some incantations to
straighten your back.

Grandfather Hmm? What's that? Cure his old grandpa's crooked
back will he? (*laughs and then stops to ponder*) The lad
will use his great powers to straighten his old grandpa's
back?

Tarō Kaja That's what he says, sir.

Grandfather (*laughs*) Well, well! Isn't that the limit. Now isn't that
the limit! He's really done his homework. I'd be very
happy to have him straighten my back. Hurry up!
Stretch me out!

Priest Nothing to it, sir. I'll have you cured with a single
prayer.

Grandfather Ho! Splendid!

incantation (noh style)

Priest An ascetic offers an incantation.
(*moves forward and stares at his beads*)
Irataka beads, these are not.
They're just any old seeds I've rounded up and

strung together every which way,
and call irataka.
(*rolls beads in his hands*)
'Clackety, clack,' I roll them.
(*turns to grandfather*)
I raise my voice in prayer
for the stretching of my grandfather's sacroiliac.
Boron, boron, boron, boron . . .

Grandfather	How about that! He's learned some pretty fancy moves!
Tarō Kaja	Indeed he has, sir.
Grandfather	(*Little by little his back straightens out until he is bent over backward slightly.*) Ahh! Tarō Kaja! My back is stretching!
Tarō Kaja	It really is, sir!
Grandfather	Ouch! Oh, that hurts! Oh! Ow! That hurts!
Priest	(*examines the grandfather's back*) Looks fine to me. Well Tarō Kaja? How about it? Has it stretched?
Tarō Kaja	It's a miracle, sir.
Priest	Well, Grandfather? How's that?
Grandfather	(*holds onto his staff and looks distressed*) What d'you mean "how's that"? It's killing me! How long will I be stuck like this?
Priest	"How long?" This is what the expression "for life" means.
Grandfather	What? It can't be undone?
Priest	Exactly, sir.
Grandfather	I can stand it for an hour or maybe two but don't you go

throwing "for life" at me! Oooh! It hurts! It hurts! Oh! My sacroiliac! Hurry up! Bend it back!

Priest   Well, if you put it that way, sir, I can see your point. Just now I overstretched it a bit, as you can see. So, if it's all right with you, I'll bend it back as it was.

Grandfather   Oooh! Hurry! Oooh! Pray it back!

Tarō Kaja   Well, well, you're quite accomplished, sir.

Priest   Not a bit of it! Not a bit of it! Any fool could do it. Why, with my powers, I could pray an ocean dry, pray the mountains to the ground . . .

Tarō Kaja   My! That's incredible!

incantantion (noh style, dynamic mode)

Priest   (*Faces front with the beads in his hand.*)

No matter how overstretched a back,
if I pray it into the Guardian King's grasp
(*rolls the beads*)
how can a miracle fail to occur?
Boron, boron, boron, boron . . .

Grandfather   Oh! Oh! That's enough!

Tarō Kaja   Goodness! A miracle!

Grandfather   Stop! That's enough! Ouch! Ouch! It hurts! It hurts!

Priest   What's the trouble? What's wrong?

Grandfather   (*Forced over by the prayers, he drops his staff and falls suddenly to the floor in terrible pain.*)

What d'you mean, "What's wrong"? I'm bent over double! It hurts! Quick! Pray me back as I was!

Priest	(*surprised*) I guess I did go too far. Tarō Kaja!
Tarō Kaja	Yes, sir.
Priest	It's worse than it was when we started out.
Tarō Kaja	(*studies the back carefully*) Yes, sir. He's doubled over.
Priest	Hm. This is more difficult than I thought. I can't just leave him that way. Not when he's in such terrible pain. I'm going to pray. Please back me up.
Tarō Kaja	Oh, I don't know the first thing about prayers or spells or anything. I won't be of any use.
Priest	No, no. I don't mean help with the prayers. When I've got his back in exactly the right spot, I want you to support him from behind with the stick. That way he won't bend over backward again.
Tarō Kaja	That's a good idea. I'll do what I can.
Priest	It's a pretty tricky back so stay on your toes!
Tarō Kaja	(*Takes up the staff which the grandfather dropped and stands ready.*)
	You can count on me, sir.
Grandfather	Ohhh! Get on with it!

incantation (noh style, dynamic mode)

Priest	No matter how ornery a back, when I pray "i-ro-ha-ni-ho-he-to"[2] how can a miracle fail to occur? Boron, boron, boron, boron . . .
Grandfather	Ouch! It hurts! It hurts!

Priest	Tarō Kaja! Steady now!
Tarō Kaja	(*Kneels on one knee behind and to the side of the grandfather and presses the staff into the grandfather's back.*)
	I've got it, sir!
Priest	Boron, boron . . .
Grandfather	(*Makes a grab for his cane as he falls backward and the cane falls forward.*)
	Ouch! Oh! It hurts! It hurts!
Tarō Kaja	Oh dear! What's happened? He's bent way back the other way. Sir! He's bent backward again!
Priest	(*angry and upset*) Hey! I said to be careful, didn't I? This is all your fault.
Tarō Kaja	I tried my best, sir, but it was too much for me. It's such a strong back that it bent right over backwards.
Priest	Idiot! Now we're in a fine mess. It's much worse than it was!
Tarō Kaja	Yes, sir.
Priest	What'll I do?
Tarō Kaja	How can I say, sir?
Priest	Oh, grandfather?[3]
Grandfather	(*looks up at the priest*) What!
Priest	Now you're as far back as you were forward. I know its a bit odd but it'll do, won't it?

Grandfather	What! Don't be ridiculous! You expect me to stay like this for even half an hour? You enjoy making fun of an old man, do you? You're trying my patience! Hurry up! Fix me as I was! Now!
Priest	That's rather difficult. As you see, sir, your sacroiliac's been behaving badly. It simply refuses to cooperate. But I will now return it to where it was.
Grandfather	Oh! Oh! It hurts! It hurts! Get on with it! Fix it!
Priest	(*faces front*) I wonder what to do?
Tarō Kaja	Uh, sir?
Priest	What is it?
Tarō Kaja	Maybe, since your prayers are so powerful, the spells have been too effective. Couldn't you tone them down a bit?
Priest	Hmmm. Of course! That must be it! The powers of a mountain priest are enough to bring a mountain to the ground so, as you say, they'd be too much for a frail back. You're absolutely right! In fact, when has there ever been such an inspiration in all of Japan. I'm so impressed that I'm going to do as you say; I'm going to tone down my prayers. You hold on to the stick!
Tarō Kaja	Yes, sir!
Priest	Oh, grandfather! I'm going to pray you back now.
Grandfather	Cut the palaver and get on with it! I can't stand this any longer!

incantation (noh style, dynamic mode)

Priest	No matter how difficult a spine with all of its shrinking and stretching if the Buddha incarnate, a mountain priest, prays

how can it fail to spring back straight?

(Produces his beads and prays at the back.)

Boron, boron, boron boron . . .[4]

Grandfather	Ouch! That hurts! It hurts!
Tarō Kaja	*(tries to keep the staff aimed at the back)* Please, sir! That's too much!
Priest	Steady now! Boron, boron . . .
Grandfather	Ouch! Oh! That hurts! It hurts!
Tarō Kaja	You've overdone it again, sir! It's no good!
Priest	*(glances over)* I went too far again. *(faces front)* Gee, it's a problem having such powerful spells.
Grandfather	Hey, Tarō Kaja! Hand me my stick!
Tarō Kaja	What're you going to do, sir?
Grandfather	*(stands and waves his stick about)* You little fool, you!
Priest	What're you doing, sir?
Grandfather	You think you can play jokes on me, do you?
Priest	Oh no, no, please! I didn't mean to do it. Tarō Kaja! Stop him! Someone'll get hurt.
Tarō Kaja	Pardon me, sir. Pardon me, but isn't that a bit dangerous?
Grandfather	What've you got to do with it?
Tarō Kaja	Really, sir, you mustn't do this.
Grandfather	And who's going to stop me?

Priest	Now, now. Why take it that way?
Grandfather	(*chases the priest with his stick*) You're to blame for this! Have you learned your lesson?
Priest	Oh! Please forgive me!
Grandfather	(*chases the priest*) You young whippersnapper!
Priest	Tarō Kaja! Tell him I'm sorry!
Tarō Kaja	(*following sorrowfully after them*) Oh, sir, sir! Remember, "forgive and forget."
Grandfather	What'd you mean, "forgive and forget"?
Tarō Kaja	Ohh! Sir! Excuse me but someone's going to get hurt.
Grandfather	I'll teach you! You rascal!
Priest	Sir, sir! Let me go!
Grandfather	(*chases him up the bridgeway*) Catch him!
Tarō Kaja	Pardon me, sir, but that could be dangerous.
Grandfather	Oh! I'm mad! I'm furious!
Priest	Forgive me, sir! Please forgive me!
Tarō Kaja	Sir, sir! Oh no! Oh no! This is such a shame!
Grandfather	Ooh! I'm so mad! I'm really mad!
Priest	(*Exits followed by the grandfather and Tarō Kaja.*)

Forgive me, sir! Please! Let me go![5]

The Shinto Priest meets the Mountain Priest

THE SHINTO PRIEST MEETS THE MOUNTAIN PRIEST[1]

Characters

Shite:	Mountain Priest. Dressed in standard costume. He carries a traveling case of cedar tied with a length of white cloth and attached to a pole which he balances over his right shoulder. His hair is worn loose.
Ado:	Shinto Priest. Dressed in a striped underrobe; kyōgen hakama bound to the knees; a jacket; a lacquered court hat; a small sword; and a prayer wand with a white streamer attached.
Ado:	Tea Dealer. Dressed in a vest and matching long hakama. He carries a tea bowl.
Ado:	*Daikoku* statue.[2] Dressed in a daikoku mask; a gold-threaded robe under a happi coat; a three-quarter-length cloak; a robe tied at the waist with the top half worn draping down like an apron (hakama are optional); a beret; a purse in his left hand and a hammer in his right hand.[3]

Entrance music: flute, large hip drum, small shoulder drum[4]

Shinto Priest	(*Enters and stops at the shite spot where he turns to introduce himself to the audience. The tea dealer follows him on stage and seats himself before the musicians spot.*)
	I'm one of the Ise Shrine priests on my way to pay calls on my patrons as I do every year.
	(*Circles the stage.*)
	Thanks to the gods, I travel in comfort again this year, under the protection of Ise Shrine.

163

(*Stops at center stage and looks around.*)

Hmm ...There's always been a tea shop around here but ...Tea dealer! Tea dealer! Are you there?

Tea Dealer   (*The stagehand places a tea cup in his left hand.*)[5]

Oh! It's you! Welcome!

Shinto Priest   Yes. I'm making my rounds again.

Tea Dealer   Well, well, thank you for thinking of us. First, though, have a seat.

Shinto Priest   Thank you. (*seats himself on the barrel seat*) Now then, how's everyone?

Tea Dealer   We're all well.

Shinto Priest   Every morning and evening I offer prayers at the altar for you.

Tea Dealer   I'm grateful, I'm sure. May I offer you a cup of tea?

Shinto Priest   Yes, please, may I? Mmm ...excellent tea!

Tea Dealer   Would you like another cup?

Shinto Priest   No, this is fine.

Tea Dealer   Well, then, just make yourself at home.[6]

(*The mountain priest enters with his legs lifted high as if mountain climbing.*)

Mountain Priest   (*Stops at the shite spot and faces the musicians spot to sing the shidai.*)

shidai (noh style, dynamic mode)

From Mount Ōmine to Mount Kazuragi

From Mount Ōmine to Mount Kazuragi
I'm on my way back home.

(The refrain is taken up by the chorus.)[7]

back home.[8]

I'm a Haguro mountain priest from Dewa. I've just done death-defying rites on Mounts Ōmine and Kazuragi and now I'm going home.

(Begins to circle the stage to the right.)

But what's the rush? I'll take my time.

I tell you! There's no training so tough as ours. Only by austerities like sleeping in fields with only a rock or stump for a pillow, or waking up at the hour of the tiger[9]can you get to be a great mountain priest.

Gee, I haven't eaten since morning and now I'm really thirsty too. I need a drink and I don't care if it's tea or hot water. There used to be a tea shop around here. Aha! There it is over there! I'll have some tea. Hey, hey! Tea dealer!

Tea Dealer   Yes, sir?

Mountain Priest Let's have some tea.

(Performs a hiraki at the shite spot and then kneels on one knee. With his left hand he removes the travel case[10] and takes his prayer beads in his right hand.)

Tea Dealer   *(Picks up the cup and offers it with his right hand.)*

Here you are, sir.

Mountain Priest *(goes to center stage)* What? Where is it?

(*Reaches out for the tea with his left hand. Facing front, he takes it in his right hand and drinks.*)

Ow! (*spits it out*) It's scalding!

Tea Dealer   Shall I cool it down for you?

(*Takes cup in his right hand and then places it at his side with his left hand. He uses his fan to pour the tea into the cup and then tucks the fan back into his belt and offers the tea as he did earlier.*)

Here you are, sir.

Mountain Priest   (*Takes a mouthful as before and then turns on the Tea Dealer.*)

Yuck! This isn't even warm! It's nothing but water! You call yourself a tea dealer on the high road, and yet you can't even tell the difference between hot and cold?

(*Knocks the cup over with his left hand.*)

Tea Dealer   Very sorry, sir.

(*Takes up the cup as before and returns it to his side.*)

Shinto Priest   Oh! Tea Dealer! Please try to cater to him.

Tea Dealer   Of course, sir.

Mountain Priest   (*notices the Shinto priest*) What was that? Clear out!

(*Grabs the Shinto priest by the right wrist with both hands and hurls him toward the waki spot. The priest staggers and falls.*)

Shinto Priest   Hey! What d'you think you're doing!

Tea Dealer   (*to the Shinto priest*) Please, come this way.

Shinto Priest	(*Goes to upstage left and kneels on one knee.*)
	By all means.
Tea Dealer	(*to the mountain priest*) Will you have another cup?
Mountain Priest	Huh? Oh, that.
	(*Seats himself on the barrel seat and is served tea by the tea dealer. He wraps the beads around his left hand and takes the tea in his right. After drinking with both hands, he carefully returns the cup.*)
Tea Dealer	(*takes the cup in his left hand*) Won't you have some more?
Mountain Priest	Nope.
	(*Stands and walks over to his travel case.*)
Tea Dealer	(*to the Shinto priest*) Well, well. You can come back now.
	(*Takes cup in left hand and closes his fan.*)
Shinto Priest	Of course. (*returns and seats himself as before*) Goodness! That mountain priest is really something, isn't he!
Tea Dealer	You meet all kinds on the high road.
Shinto Priest	I can handle it but no one else could.
Tea Dealer	You're absolutely right. You handled him very well.
	(*Both perform a hiraki.*)
Mountain Priest	You can't let a thing like that go by. After all, he's got no principles or he wouldn't have acted like that. You've got to let people like that know where you stand from the first.

(Glances to the right and sees the Shinto priest seated again on the barrel seat. He faces front.)

Well! How d'you like that! He's up on that seat again! Now what? Hah! I can put a stop to that!

(Tucks the travel case under his arm and strides over to the Shinto priest. Grabs the priest's right wrist and forces the pole of the travel case onto his right shoulder.)

Now, stand!

(Pulls the Shinto priest to his feet and drags him over to center stage.)

Shinto Priest   *(wobbles forward)* Help! What d'you think you're doing?

Mountain Priest   You gonna make something of it?

Shinto Priest   Oh, tea dealer! Please stop him!

Tea Dealer   *(stands)* What's going on here? Hold on now. Hold on.

(Places himself between them and grabs both their arms.)

Mountain Priest   What d'you mean "hold on"? This bum has got to carry my case until dark.

Tea Dealer   Why, I've never heard the like! If it's the law, he'll have to, of course. But, for now, let me take care of it for you.

Mountain Priest   Oh no! I don't need any of your "taking care of it" stuff. He's got to carry it.

Tea Dealer   Now, now. As long as I'm here, leave it to me please.

Mountain Priest   All right, if that's what you want, but hurry up!

Tea Dealer   Certainly.

                *(Carries the case in both hands. Facing center stage, he
                puts it down and approaches the Shinto priest.)* [11]

                Oh, sir! Sir! I know this sounds strange but do Shinto
                priests have to obey "carrying laws" when they meet
                mountain priests?

Shinto Priest   *(Places his prayer wand over his right shoulder and
                returns to center stage.)*

                What? That's ridiculous! Just ridiculous! What
                "carrying laws"? Please tell him that I refuse to carry
                anything for him.

Tea Dealer   You refuse?

                (Approaches the Mountain Priest.)

                Excuse me. Hello? I asked but he said to say that he
                refuses. He says there's no such thing as "carrying
                laws."

Mountain Priest What! He refuses?

Tea Dealer   That's right.

Mountain Priest Who does he think he is! Even the high and mighty,
                whatever their rank, kneel down before a mountain priest
                just out of the mountains. That scum of the priesthood
                dares to set himself up on a throne before my very eyes?
                He must be crazy! Tell him he's got to carry my chest
                until nightfall as punishment.

Tea Dealer   Yes, sir. *(turns to the Shinto priest)* Did you hear that?

Shinto Priest   I most certainly did. There's no question of high or low
                at a tea shop on the high road. I've never so much as
                nodded to a mountain porter before.[12] Not only that, but
                he's a complete stranger to me. Doesn't he know that a

priest is a priest and a mountain priest, a mountain priest?

Tea Dealer   You do have a point. (*turns to the mountain priest*) I told him exactly what you said and his answer was that at tea shops on the high road there is no such thing as high or low. Besides, he's never met you before, and even if he had, he's never so much as nodded to a mountain porter. He said, "Doesn't he know that priests are priests and mountain priests, mountain priests?

Mountain Priest   The bum! That scum of the priesthood puts me down in one word as a "porter?" Me? A holy mountain priest? Mountain priests climb up Ōmine and Kazuragi and say spells for all mankind. Why, I can even pray a bird down from the sky. Ask him what miracles he can perform.

Tea Dealer   Yes, sir. (*to the Shinto priest*) Did you hear that?

Shinto Priest   Indeed I did and it may be that mountain priests climb up the Ōmine and Kazuragi mountains and chant incantations for all mankind but, after all, that's their job. Lots of miracles occur when I pray too. But if you tell him that, it'll only make matters worse. Let me slip out the back.

Tea Dealer   Just a moment! You've seen what sort he is. If I let you sneak out, there'll be hell to pay. What I think is that since we're not getting anywhere this way, we should have a contest.

Shinto Priest   What sort of contest?

Tea Dealer   I have a daikoku statue made by a certain artist.[13] Both of you will pray to it and the one to whom it turns, wins. If you win, he'll carry your wand or if he wins, you'll have to carry his case.

Shinto Priest   That's no good.

Tea Dealer   And why not?

Shinto Priest	Mountain priests are always calling out spirits but we never do anything like that.
Tea Dealer	Never mind. From where I sit it's you who are the righteous one. Whereas that mountain priest is completely immoral. As they say, "The gods come to the virtuous," so you've got nothing to worry about. You're bound to win. Just pray with all your might.
Shinto Priest	Well, if you put it that way, all right. Please tell the mountain priest what the plan is.
Tea Dealer	Yes, of course. *(turns to the mountain priest)* Hey, hey! You there! We're not going to resolve anything this way, so why don't we have a contest.
Mountain Priest	What? Hey you! What's this about needing a contest? He's got to take what's coming to him, that's all. We don't need you to decide anything. I'll make him carry it!
	(Heads for the case and tries to force it on the Shinto priest.)
Tea Dealer	*(Approaches the mountain priest to stop him.)*
	Hold on! Hold on! I'll handle this. If you refuse to participate, then it just proves that you're too much of a sinner.
Mountain Priest	What's that? I'm a sinner?
Tea Dealer	That's right.
Mountain Priest	*(returns to his original spot)* Oh, all right. What're we competing for?
Tea Dealer	I've got a daikoku statue by a certain artist. Both of you pray and the one to whom it turns, wins. The priest carries your chest or you carry the prayer wand.

Mountain Priest   What? Pray to a daikoku statue?

Tea Dealer   That's right.

Mountain Priest   (*guffaws*) What a joke! All a daikoku does is to bring luck to the house. What would a daikoku have to do with this? Anyway, we mountain priests only pray to the great Fudō. Who ever heard of us praying to anything so stupid as a daikoku?[14]

Tea Dealer   That's a different story from the one you've been feeding us! You said you could pray a bird down from the sky. If you refuse then you lose.

Mountain Priest   What? If I don't pray, I lose?

Tea Dealer   That's about it.

Mountain Priest   What's the big deal? Get it out here. Quick!

Tea Dealer   Yes, sir. (*goes to the Shinto priest*) Excuse me. I'm going to fetch the daikoku.

Shinto Priest   Hurry! Bring him out.

Tea Dealer   Of course, sir. (*exits to get the daikoku*)

(*In the interval the Shinto priest attempts to steal past the mountain priest but is stopped by the angry glares and posturing of the mountain priest.*)[15]

Tea Dealer   (*Leads the daikoku on stage to front center. He grasps the daikoku with both hands and seats him on the barrel seat. The tea dealer stands between the Shinto priest and the daikoku.*) [16]

Here we are! Here we are! Here's the daikoku!

Shinto Priest   Well! I must say that's a splendid daikoku!

(*Turns to the daikoku and waves his prayer wand by grasping it in both hands and shaking it in the air. He then returns it to his shoulder.*)

Mountain Priest   That's some daikoku, all right!

(*Turns carelessly toward the daikoku and then backs away, scared.*)

Tea Dealer   And now, the prayers!

Shinto Priest   After the honorable mountain priest.

Mountain Priest   Oh, no you don't. You two are in cahoots. Let's see you do it!

Shinto Priest   Oh, after you, please!

Mountain Priest   What! When I say "pray" then you'd better...

(*He thrusts his left leg forward with a thud, threateningly.*)

Tea Dealer   (*to the Shinto priest*) Now, now. Why not begin?

Shinto Priest   (*intimidated*) If you wish.

(*Turns to the daikoku and waves his wand. Then, taking the wand in his left hand, he raises it in prayer and faces front. With the wand grasped in both hands, he begins to chant.*)

Shinto prayer (noh style, melodic mode.)

I pray to thee, oh gods, again and again[17]
Humbly I beseech thee.
The Goddess Amaterasu
is the ancestral goddess of our land.
Never has she failed to grant our prayers
from the time of her descent
to the land of Ise
over the waters of Isuzugawa in Doai.[18]
I make my supplication to the gods.

> Bless me with thy presence.
> Bestow thy mercy upon me.
> I pray to thee, again and again.
> I pray to thee, again and again.[19]

Tea Dealer   (*Looking at the daikoku which has swung around to face the Shinto priest.*)

A miracle! A miracle! We already have the winner. Now you'll have to carry his wand![20]

Mountain Priest   Wait a minute! I haven't even had my turn yet!

Tea Dealer   Well, of course. That's true. Go ahead! Pray!

Mountain Priest   Right.

incantation (noh style, dynamic mode)

> A mountain priest is called a mountain priest
> because he sleeps in the mountains.
>
> —Did you catch that?—

Tea Dealer   Yes, indeed, that must be so.

Mountain Priest

incantation (continued)

> A tokin is a foot-long piece of cloth
> folded into pleats and popped on the bean
> and therefore called a tokin!

Tea Dealer   Ah.

Mountain Priest   Irataka prayer beads—

(*Performs a hiraki to the right and studies the beads.*)

these are not.

They're just any old beads I've strung together
and call 'irataka.'
If I offer a prayer,
how can I fail to have a miracle?[21]

(*Rolls the beads.*)

Boron, boron, boron . . .

(*Wraps the beads around his wrist and turns to the daikoku. At the conclusion of the prayer, the daikoku turns toward the mountain priest. The mountain priest is delighted and prays again, but this time the daikoku whips around to face the Shinto priest.*)[22]

Tea Dealer   (*sees the daikoku spin around to face the Shinto priest*)
                  Well! This is altogether different!

Shinto Priest   It sure is.

Mountain Priest   (*grabs the daikoku's sleeve*)

                  Boron, boron, boron . . .

                  (*The daikoku strikes him on the head with his hammer.*)

Tea Dealer   Ah ha! That settles it! You carry the wand!

Shinto Priest   It's all decided! It's decided!

Mountain Priest   Uh, uh. Nothing's settled yet. Wait a minute! Wait!

Shinto Priest   For what?

Mountain Priest   This is a very bad daikoku. I'm going to pray again, and
                  this time, you'll pray with me.

Shinto Priest   Oh no! Oh no! There's no need for us to pray together!

Mountain Priest   So, you refuse, do you?

(*Thrusts out his left leg and shakes his right fist aggressively. The frightened Shinto priest backs away.*)

Tea Dealer   Now, now. Couldn't you pray with him?

Shinto Priest   I suppose so.

(*As before he waves the wand and begins to pray.*)

Shinto prayer (noh style, melodic mode.)

I trust myself to the gods.
Reveal thy presence to me once again.
(*shakes the wand up and down*)
I pray to thee, again and again.
I pray to thee, again and again.
I pray to thee, again and again.

(*Dances from foot to foot as before.*)

Mountain Priest   (*Prays with hands clasped together and wrapped in his beads.*)[23]

incantation (noh style, dynamic mode.)

No matter how evil a daikoku you are
if I offer just one prayer
(*rubs beads*)
how can a miracle fail to occur?
Boron, boron, boron . . .

(*Turns to face the daikoku and prays without the beads. He offers a prayer but the daikoku turns to the Shinto priest. The mountain priest is very displeased and prays louder to no avail. The mountain priest then approaches the daikoku as he prays and suddenly grabs the daikoku's right sleeve and swings him around. The daikoku responds by knocking him down with his mallet.[24] This happens several times, with the daikoku turning back to the Shinto priest each time. By the third or fifth time, the daikoku chases the mountain priest around the stage with his mallet raised and finally chases him off.*)[25]

—

The Snail

THE SNAIL[1]

Characters

    Shite: Mountain priest. Dressed in usual costume with a conch shell hanging from his right shoulder and with prayer beads.

    Ado: Father. Dressed in long hakama and matching vest.

    Ado: Son. Dressed in short hakama and matching vest.

Priest   *(Enters with legs lifted high as if mountain climbing and stops at the shite spot. He turns to face the musicians spot.)*[2]

On his way down from the three peaks
On his way down from the three peaks
A mountain priest is grand indeed. *(faces audience)*
I'm a mountain priest from Mount Haguro in Dewa. I've been up Ōmine and Kazuragi and now that I've done death-defying rites, I'm on my way home. But what's the rush? I'll just stroll along.

(Circles the stage.)

I tell you! There's no other training as hard as ours! Sometimes, I've only a rock or log for a pillow. I turn in at the hour of the rat[3] and I'm up by the hour of the tiger[4] But it's only by undergoing such tough training that you can call yourself a mountain priest.

(Stops at the shite spot.)

I've gotten this far and now I'm beat. And sleepy too! I could use a nap.

(Gazes toward the waki spot.)

Ah ha! Those bushes over there should do. I'll crawl in and take a look around.

181

(*Uses his hands to part the branches and, calling out "ei, ei," he leaps over a stream into the thicket.*)

Yes! This'll do fine. Now then, I'm going to catch a few winks.

(*Stands in front of the musicians spot, upstage center, and flops down facing the waki spot, using his right arm for a pillow.*)

Ahhh! This is heavenly! Just heavenly! I'll take a short nap.

Father   (*Enters, followed by Tarō. Tarō kneels forward of the shite spot. The father announces himself at center stage.*)

I live here. My uncle's got a chronic complaint and he's constantly bothering me with his aches and pains. It's gotten so that even the master is annoyed. Today, my uncle just had another attack and is feeling worse than ever. He claims that snails would cure his pains so I guess I'll send my son out to look for one.[5]

(*Faces upstage and performs a hiraki.*)

Hey, hey! Where is everybody?

Tarō   (*stands at the shite spot*) That sounds like father. (*turns to face the father*) I'm here, sir! Did you want something?

Father   You know your uncle has just had another bad bout. I'm quite worried. What'll we do?

Tarō   Of course, he's so old, we can't help worrying.

Father   That's right, my boy. They say that a snail might cure him. I want you to go and get one for me.

Tarō   Yes, sir, but I've never seen a snail so I wouldn't know what to look for.

Father	That's ridiculous! How could you not know what a snail is? All right. I'll tell you what to look for and you go and get it.
Tarō	Yes, of course, sir.
Father	First of all, snails crawl out of the ground and live in bushes.
Tarō	Ah ha! Then all I need to do is to hunt in some bushes and I'll find one.
Father	Yes, yes. Bushes are full of them.
Tarō	All right. But what do snails look like?
Father	Their heads are pitch black and they have horns.
Tarō	I see, sir.
Father	They have shells on their backs. Oh yes, and some of the old ones are incredibly big. Don't forget now!
Tarō	I've got it, sir. I'm off to hunt snails.
Father	On your way!
Tarō	Yes, sir!
Father	Go on!
Tarō	Sir!

(Turns and takes four steps forward from the shite spot.)

Too bad! Uncle's worse. What a pity. I'd better hurry and find him that snail.

(Circles the stage.)

It would really be great if a snail turned up right away. He said they're found in bushes so I'll try a bush.

(*Stops at the shite spot and turns to face the waki spot.*)

Ah ha! I'll try that bush over there and see if there's a snail.

(*Mimes crossing a stream, and as he jumps he catches sight of the mountain priest.*)

Why! There's a black-headed creature right over there. I'll go and ask if he's a snail.

(*Wakes up the mountain priest and then withdraws downstage to wait.*)

Hello! Hello there! Where are you from?

Priest   Ahh. That felt good! Just what I needed! I slept like a baby.

(*Slowly, he stands, takes up his beads in his right hand, and goes downstage.*)

Tarō   (*turns to the mountain priest*) Hello, sir! Hello!

Priest   What d'you want?

Tarō   Where are you from, sir?

Priest   I was tired and lay down for a nap. Do you own this land?

Tarō   Oh no. I'm not the owner. I just wanted to ask you something.

Priest   Yes?

Tarō   I don't mean to be rude, but could you be a snail?

Priest	What? Am I a snail?
Tarō	Yes, sir.
Priest	What a strange question. Why do you ask?
Tarō	Well, I've heard that snails have black heads and live in bushes. So, when I saw your black head, I wondered.
Priest	Hmm . . . That's logical. Why are you looking for a snail?
Tarō	You see, I have this uncle who suffers from a chronic complaint and he's just had another bad attack. Even the master is getting annoyed. Someone suggested that snails might cure him so I came to you.
Priest	Of course! I see now. Wait there a moment.
Tarō	Yes sir.
Priest	(*Goes to the waki spot and laughs.*)
	What a dummy! There are some real fools in this world. He takes one look at my head and asks if I'm a snail! I'll pretend to be one and tease him a bit. (*turns to the boy*) Hey! Hey there!
Tarō	Yes, sir?
Priest	You should be more careful when you speak of such important matters! It so happens that I am the greatest snail in the world.
Tarō	Just what I thought! I asked because I noticed your black head. I'm lucky to have found you so soon. But I've also been told that snails have shells on their backs. What about you? Have you got one?
Priest	What? A shell?

Tarō	Yes, sir.
Priest	Well, well! You're a smart boy! Actually I do have a shell. Would you like to see it?
Tarō	Yes, sir. I would.
Priest	That's simple.
	(Turns his back to the boy and faces the waki spot. He takes his right sleeve in his left hand and holds it under his arm so that it looks like a shell from behind.)
	Here it is! Here it is!
Tarō	*(watches the mountain priest)* I can see it!
Priest	It's a splendid shell, don't you think?
Tarō	It's simply enormous! But I've also heard that snails have horns. Where are yours?
Priest	What? Horns?
Tarō	Yes, sir.
Priest	*(looks perplexed)* Of course, of course. I can show you my horns. Just a minute.
Tarō	Yes sir.
Priest	*(Goes to the waki spot.)*
	Let's see. These horns have me stumped! What'll I do? I know! *(turns to the boy)* Hey! You there! You there!
Tarō	Yes, sir?
Priest	So you want to see my horns, do you?

Tarō	I do, sir.
Priest	Then, I'll show them to you, but whatever you do, don't tell anyone!
Tarō	I promise, sir.
Priest	(*Turns his back to the boy and pushes his mantle up over his shoulders.*)
	Get ready now! My horns are coming out! Look! Look!
Tarō	Gosh!
Priest	(*Pulls the mantle back into place and faces the boy.*)
	How about it? I'll bet my horns came out.
Tarō	Oh yes, sir! They did! I've also heard that some snails live so long that they grow to be very big. You're certainly big!
Priest	You'll never find another like me no matter how long or far you search. You're lucky you found me so soon.
Tarō	I sure am, sir. I can't imagine being luckier. All right. Let's go back to my house now.
Priest	You know, I'd really like to oblige you but I haven't a moment free. All the old people in the area are sick. Sorry, but I can't come with you.
Tarō	That's a terrible shame. We had such a lucky meeting and all. Please come with me.
Priest	When you put it like that, it does seem a shame. All right. But I can't just take off like that.
Tarō	You can't?

Priest   I've got to have rhythm.

Tarō   That shouldn't be too hard, should it?

Priest   Not at all. Not at all. Nothing to it. You start off by
              chanting, "Since it neither rains nor blows, if you don't
              come out, I'll crush your shell; if you don't come out I'll
              crush your shell!" Then I'll join in with "Come out,
              come out, snail, snail; come out, come out, snail, snail!"[6]
              And we'll move along to the beat.

Tarō   Sounds simple enough. Let me try it.

Priest   Yes, go ahead.

Tarō   All right. (*begins to chant*) Since it neither rains nor
              blows, if you don't come out, I'll crush your shell; I'll
              crush your shell-l-l! How's that?

Priest   Oh! That's it! You've got it! Now then, let's go! Come
              on!

              (*Wraps his beads around his fist.*)

Tarō   Yes, sir.

              (*Takes out his fan and beats a rhythm on his palm as he
              dances from one foot to the other.*)

              Since it neither rains nor blows
              If you don't come out, I'll crush your shell!
              If you don't come out, I'll crush your shell!

Priest   (*Circles the stage.*)

              Come out, come out!
              Snail, snail!
              Come out, come out!
              Snail, snail-l-l-l![7]

Tarō   (*Keeps time with his fan as he hops from foot to foot in place.*)

Since it neither rains nor blows
If you don't come out, I'll crush your shell!
If you don't come out, I'll crush your shell!

Priest   Come out, come out!
            Snail, snail!
            Come out, come out!
            Snail, snail-l-l!

Tarō   Since it neither rains nor blows,
            If you don't come out, I'll crush your shell.
            If you don't come out, I'll crush your shell!

Priest   Come out, come out!
            Snail, snail!
            Come out, come out!
            Snail, snail-l-l-l!

Father   (*Enters and stops at the first pine on the bridgeway.*)

            It's very late. I expected my son back with a snail by
            now. I've had to come out looking for him. What can he
            be up to?

            (*Enters the stage and, catching sight of the child, he
            retreats to the bridgeway.*)

            What's going on here? There he is over there larking
            about! Hey! Hey there! Hey boy!

            (*Performs a hiraki at the first pine on the bridgeway.*)

Tarō   (*Turns to his father at the shite spot but the mountain
            priest tugs on his sleeve.*)

            Father! Did you come looking for me?

Father   What on earth are you doing here?

| Tarō | What should I be doing? Why, I'm bring home a snail. |

Tarō   What should I be doing? Why, I'm bring home a snail.

Father   What? You're bringing home a snail?

Tarō   That's right, sir.

Father   What're you talking about?

Tarō   (*glances over at the mountain priest*) That's the snail, over there.

Father   Oh, for heaven's sake!

Priest   Sing, sing!

(*Dances past the child and then they dance toward each other, chanting.*)

Tarō   (*hops toward the mountain priest*) I am! I am!

Since it neither rains nor blows

(*Mountain priest stamps.*)

If you don't come out, I'll crush your shell.

(*Priest stamps twice.*)

If you don't come out, I'll crush your shel-l-l-l.

(*Priest stamps twice.*)

Priest   (*slides to the left*) Come out, come out! (*stamps to the right*)

Snail, (*stamps left*)

snail. (*stamps twice to the right*)

Come out, come out! Snail, (*stamps right, left, right*)

snail. (*stamps*)

Come out, come out! (*stamps and jumps to the right*)

Snail, (*stamps and jumps*)

snail. (*stamps left and right*)

Tarō   (*Stands still. The mountain priest notices and listens as the father speaks and then tugs on Tarō's sleeve.*)

See! His head is black.[8]

Father   What's the boy babbling about? It seems he's been tricked. (*goes to the shite spot*) Hey, hey! You there!

Tarō   What?

Father   So, he's made a fool of you. What d'you think he is? He's a mountain priest!

Tarō   What do you mean? He's a snail! (*looks at the mountain priest*) Look! His head is black . . .

Priest   (*Sings "come out, come out! Snail, snail . . ."*)

Now then, the beat, the beat!

Tarō   Of course. (*sings and dances*)

Since it neither rains nor blows
If you don't come out, I'll crush your shell.
If you don't come out, I'll crush your shell.

Priest   Come out, come out. (*stamps right*)

Snail, (*stamps left*)

Snail. (*stamps right, left, right*)

Come out, come out. (*stamps*)

Snail, (*stamps right, left*)

snail-l-l-l! (*stamps right, left*)

Tarō   Since it

(*Mountain priest stamps left, right.*)[9]

neither rains nor blows,
If you don't come out, I'll crush your shell!

Father   (*at the shite spot*) What a dolt! He's made a complete fool of you!

Tarō   Huh?

Father   You little idiot. That's a mountain priest; a bum!

Tarō   Sir? You're sure he's a mountain priest?

Father   Ohh! I'll handle this. You, get along home. Get along with you. (*roughly*) Hey! You there!

(*Turns to the mountain priest and starts toward him. The priest tugs at the child's sleeve and calls out, "sing, sing!" The father yells roughly.*)

Hey! You there!

Priest   What d'you want?

(*Lets go of Tarō's sleeve and retreats upstage.*)

Tarō   What're you going to do, father?

Priest   Come on! Sing! Sing!

Father   You should be ashamed of yourself! You've made a real fool of my boy, haven't you!

Priest	What d'you mean, "made a fool of him?"
Father	Ohhhh, you!
Priest	Come out (*stamps right*)
	Come out! Snail, snail! (*stamps right*)
	Come out, come out! Snail, snail!

(*Thrusts his right fist forward, then his left fist and leg, and then his right again. The last time, with his right fist thrust forward and raising his right leg, he chants "Come out, come out! Snail, snail!" and, for a moment, hypnotizes both the father and Tarō. He pulls them after him with the hypnotic rhythm of his chant.*)[10]

Tarō	(*watches the priest's fist*) I did see him push out his horns. Just watch!

(*He begins to dance and sing as if hypnotized by the priest and the father follows inspite of himself.*)

Since it neither rains nor blows
Crush the shell, crush the shell!

Father	(*at the shite spot*) I can't bear anymore of this. What a mess he's gotten himself into. Hey, boy! Didn't I tell you he's nothing but a no good bum and still you're babbling away!
Tarō	Then you're sure he's just a bad man?
Father	Of course I am. Can't you see it, yourself? Get on home with you. Oh, no! Now where'd he go?[11]
Tarō	He was here a minute ago.

(*Father and son hunt for the mountain priest, who seems to elude them.*)

There he is! There he is!

Priest

(*Thrusts his right fist beneath the father's nose.*)

Come out, come out! Snail, snail-l-l!

(*Laughs and goes to the first pine on the bridgeway where he performs a hiraki. When he sees the father and Tarō coming after him, he begins chanting again.*)

Come out, come out! Snail, snail!

(*Thrusts out his right leg and fist and then his left.*)

Come out, come out! Snail, snail! (*laughs*)

Father

Now what do I do?

Priest

Here I am! Here I am!

Father

Quick! Catch him! Catch the rat!

Priest

Oh, oh! (*stamps*) This is fun!

Tarō

Quick! Catch him!

Priest

Come out, come out! Snail, snail! (*exits, laughing*)

Father

He's still at it! Where is everybody? Catch that priest! Catch him! Hurry! Catch him! You'll be sorry! You'll be sorry!

ENDNOTES

FOREWORD: (pp. 3-11)

[1]The essay is included in Tanizaki Jun'ichiro, *Tsuki to kyōgenshi* (Tokyo: Chōū kōron, 1981). The quote is on page 23.

[2]Shigeyama Sensaku, *Kyōgen hachijūnen* (Kyoto: Miyako shuppansha, 1951), p. 211.

[3]For an attempt at thematic organization, see Hata Tōru, "Kyakuhon ron," *Geinō no kagaku geinō ronkō*, vol. 2 (Tokyo: Kitamura, 1977).

[4]See Yokomichi Mario's introductions to the two volumes of *Yōkyokushū* in Nihon koten bungaku taikei, vols. 40, 41 (Tokyo: Iwanami shoten, 1980), pp. 14-25. The concept of a performance pattern is quite different for a noh play, in which the shodan are integral to the play's structure and not used specifically to identify the character such as we would expect in kyōgen.

[5]Koyama Hiroshi, ed., *Kyōgenshū*, vol. 1, Nihon koten bungaku taikei, vol. 42 (Tokyo: Iwanami shoten, 1972). p. 243.

[6]Ibid., p.124.

[7]*Kyōgenki* (1660), *Zokukyōgenki* (1700), and *Kyōgenkishū* (1730), containing fifty plays each. In *Kyōgen zenshū* (Tokyo: Kokumin bunko kankōkai, 1914), and in *Kyōgenki*, Nihon bungaku taikei, vol. 22 (Tokyo: Kaibundo, 1931).

[8]In Furukawa Hisashi, ed., *Kyōgen kohon nishū* (Tokyo: Wanya shoten, 1968).

[9]In Ikeda Hiroshi et al., eds., *Kyōgenshū no kenkyū* (Tokyo: Hyōgensha, 1972).

[10]Copies (1975 reprint) available in the Tenri Library at Tenri University in Osaka. However, I have also referred to Taguchi Kazuo, *Kyōgen ronkō* (Tokyo: Miyai shoten, 1977), pp. 82-86 for excerpts of *Persimmons,* and to Ikeda Hiroshi, *Kokyōgen daihon no hattatsu ni kanshite no shoshiteki kenkyū* (Tokyo: Kazama shoten, 1967), pp. 165-166 for *The Crab.*

[11]Sasano Ken, ed., *Noh kyōgen,* 3 vols., Iwanami bunko (Tokyo: Iwanami shoten, 1978).

[12]Yoshida Kōichi, ed., *Izumiryū kyōgenshū,* 20 vols., Koten bunko bon (Tokyo, 1955).

[13]Furukawa Hisashi, ed., *Kyōgenshū,* 3 vols., Nihon koten zensho, vols. 43-45 (Tokyo: Asahi shimbun, 1970).

[14]Koyama Hiroshi, *Kyōgenshū,* vols. 1-2.

[15]In Nonomura Kaizō et al., eds., *Kyōgen sanbyakubanshū* (Tokyo: Toyamabō, 1938).

[16]In Nonomura Kaizō et al. eds., *Kyōgen shūsei* (Tokyo: Nōgaku shorin, 1974).

[17]Elam Keir, *The Semiotics of Theatre and Drama* (London: Menthuen and Co. Ltd., 1980).

TRANSFORMATIONS: (pp. 15-23)

[1]I use the term *medieval* advisedly, to cover the period from the fifteenth through the sixteenth century.

[2]William R. LaFleur, *The Karma of Words* (Berkeley: University of California Press, 1983), p. 30.

[3]Ibid., pp. 35-37.

[4] For a more complete discussion on the nature of belief in myths, see Paul Veyne, *Did the*

Greeks Believe in Their Myths (Chicago: University of Chicago Press, 1988).

[5]Other examples of this type of humor can be found in *Seisuishō*, a collection of humorous stories from the fifteenth and sixteenth centuries. See, Suzuki Tōzō, ed., *Seisuishō: sengoku no warai banashi*, Tōyō bunko, vol. 31 (Tokyo: Heibonsha, 1981).

[6]Satake Akihiro, *Gekokujō no bungaku* (Tokyo: Chikuma shobō, 1982), pp. 137-138. (Satake refers the reader to an article by Kohitsu Matsuo entitled "Kyōgen: Medieval Humor in the Mountain Priest Plays," *Kokubungaku kenkyū*, vol. 19. According to Satake, Kohitsu argues that the *Tenshō bon* text does not specify either a woodcutter or a thief as characters in the play *The Lunchbox Thief*. Therefore, he believes that the thief is meant to be one of the mountain priests who appear as a group in this version. From this, Satake concludes that the mountain priest is being ridiculed in this as well as in the other plays in the mountain priest category. Be that as it may, Kohitsu's article does not support Satake's thesis that the mountain priests' prayers inevitably fail in some way. In the *Tenshō bon* version, as in later versions, the mountain priest successfully ousts the thief.)

[7]Koyama Hiroshi, ed., *Kyōgenshū*, vol. 1, Nihon koten bungaku taikei, vol. 42 (Tokyo: Iwanami shoten, 1972), pp. 5, 6.

[8]Ibid., pp. 280-284. (All the following quotes from *Nari agari* are from these pages.)

[9]For other examples of this type of transformation in tale literature, see Satake, *Gekokujō no bungaku*, pp. 37-63. There are examples of the *nari agari* phenomenon in *Issun bōshi*, and *Monogusa Tarō*. For an excellent translation of *Monogusa Tarō* and a variant of the Issun bō shi theme, *Ko otoko no sōshi*, see Virginia Skord, *Tales of Tears and Laughter* (Honolulu: University of Hawaii Press, 1991). See also Marian Ury, *Tales of Times Now Past* (Berkeley: University of California Press, 1979) for lively translations of a selection of tales from the *Konjaku monogatari* containing Buddhist stories of transformation.

[10]Quoted in Koyama Hiroshi, *Kyōgenshū*, vol.1, pp. 7-8.

[11]*Hito wo uma* was dropped from the Ōkura school repertory in the Meiji period, and is no longer performed by the Izumi school.

[12]See Victor Turner, *The Ritual Process* (Ithaca: Cornell University Press, 1966), and *Dramas, Fields and Metaphors* (Ithaca: Cornell University Press, 1974). See also Mikhail Bakhtin, *Rabelais and His World* (Bloomington: Indiana University Press, 1984). Bakhtin argues that the clowns and fools of the European medieval culture of humor partake of the carnival spirit characterized by a suspension of all hierarchical precedence during carnival time. In other words, they are allowed a certain comic license because they exist outside of official culture.

[13]See Nihon bungaku kenkyū shiryō kankōkai, *Yōkyoku kyōgen* (Tokyo: Yūseidō, 1981), pp.190-210. See also Hayashiya Tatsusaburō, *Chūsei bunka no kichō* (Tokyo: Iwanami, 1973); *Chūsei geinōshi no Kenkyū* (Tokyo: Iwanami, 1976); "Chūsei geinō no shakaiteki kiban," *Bungaku* 16 (December 1948): 707-715; "Kyōgen ni okeru warai," *Bungaku* 21 (August 1953): 797-802; and "Momoyama jidai igo no nō, kyōgen," *Kokubungaku: kaishaku to kanshō* 269 (October 1958): 35-39. See also Matsumoto Shinpachirō, "Kyōgen ni okeru toshi to nōson," *Bungaku* 16 (December 1948): 723-732.

[14] LaFleur, p. 136.

TRACKING THE ELUSIVE COMIC ACTOR: (pp. 25-39)

[1]*Sarugaku* was a popular form of variety entertainment in the Kamakura and Muromachi periods and included comic skits as well as song and dance. It is thought to have originated in a form of court entertainment (*sangaku*) brought to Japan from China in the eighth century.

[2]*Dengaku* was a popular form of entertainment in the Kamakura and Muromachi periods which came to resemble sarugaku in content. It originated in an indigenous form of agricultural ritual dance, called *taue* or *onda*, which mimicked the motions of rice-planting and was accompanied by rice planting songs. For further information see P. G. O'Neill, *Early Nō Drama* (London: Lund Humphries, 1958), pp. 85-94.

[3]Ando Tsunejiro et al., *Kyōgen sōran* (Tokyo: Nōgaku shorin, 1973), p. 5. See also Sakanishi Shio, *The Ink Smeared Lady* (Rutland, Vermont: Charles E. Tuttle, 1960), p. 5.

[4] O'Neill, *Early Nō Drama*, p. 2.

[5]This type of parody of religious figures is found in early Christian church ceremonies as well, "The Feast of the Ass," for example, and can be understood as a temporary passage into a liminal mode of being from which the practitioners return to reassert church authority. Victor Turner gives a convincing analysis of this phenomenon in *The Ritual Passage* (Ithaca, New York: Cornell University Press, 1966.)

[6]Nishikawa Kyōtarō, *Bugaku Masks*, trans. Monica Bethe (New York: Kōdansha International Ltd. 1978), p. 48.

[7]D. E. Mills, *A Collection of Tales from Uji* (Cambridge: Cambridge University Press, 1970), pp. 240-241.

[8]See Mikhail Bakhtin, *Rabelais and His World* (Bloomington: Indiana University Press, 1984.)

[9]Koyama Hiroshi, ed., *Kyōgenshū,* vol. 1, Nihon koten bungaku taikei, vol. 42 (Tokyo: Iwanami shoten, 1972), p. 13.

[10]Ibid., p. 13.

[11]As translated in Thomas Rimer and Yamazaki Masakazu, *On the Art of the Nō Drama* (Princeton: Princeton University Press, 1984), p. 170.

[12]Ibid., p. 170.

[13]This role is known as the *katari ai*. The second main category of aikyōgen is the *ashirai ai* which is an active role within noh and is more common in later noh plays.

[14]Rimer, *On the Art of the Nō Drama*, p. 227.

[15]Koyama Hiroshi, *Noh kyōgen: kyōgen no sekai*, vol. 5 (Tokyo: Iwanami shoten, 1987), p. 10.

[16]Ibid., p. 11.

[17]Ibid., pp. 9, 20.

[18]Rimer, *On the Art of the Nō Drama*, p. 234.

[19]Ibid., p. 232.

[20]There is some question as to whether *Mimihiki* was composed by Hideyoshi and is the

200   Endnotes

forerunner of today's *Kuchimonomane*, as stated by Andō Tsunejirō et al., *Kyōgen sōran*, p.
18, or whether *Mimihiki* might be the forerunner of *Igui* as suggested by Furukawa Hisashi et
al., *Kyōgen jiten jikōhen* (Tokyo: Tokyodo shuppan, 1976), p. 343.

[21]Koyama Hiroshi, ed., *Noh kyōgen*, vol. 5, p. 152.

[22]Genzaemon is said to have been the nephew of Mangorō, and Yozaemon his disciple.

[23]Koyama Hiroshi, "Kotei zen no kyōgen 1," *Kokugo to kokubungaku*, 318 (October 1950):
71-77.

[24]Koyama Hiroshi, ed., *Noh kyōgen*, vol. 5, p. 155. For a complete record of the performance,
see Ikeda Hiroshi et al., eds., *Kyōgen*, Nihon shomin bunka shiryō shūsei, vol. 4 (Tokyo:
Sanichi shobō, 1975.), pp. 281-293.

[25]Koyama Hiroshi, *Noh kyōgen*, vol. 5, pp. 155-156.

[26]James Brandon, *Kabuki Five Classic Plays* (Cambridge: Harvard University Press, 1975),
pp. 1-5.

[27]Dorothy Shibano, *"Kyōgen": The Comic as Drama* (Michigan: University of Michigan
Microfilms International, 1973), pp. 3, 19.

[28]Koyama Hiroshi, "Kotei zen no kyōgen," pp. 71-77.

[29]The Sagi school's explanation is somewhat different. It claims it adopted the name "Sagi"
because of the troupe's skill in performing the kyōgen *Sagi* (found in *Kyōhō Yasunori bon*).
See Koyama Hiroshi, ed., *Noh kyōgen*, vol. 5, p. 158.

[30]Ōkura Toraaki, "Waranbegusa," in Nishio Minoru et al., eds., *Yōkyoku kyōgen*, Kokugo
kokubungaku kenkyūshi taisei, vol. 8 (Tokyo: Sanseidō, 1977), p. 517.

[31]Yonekura Toshiaki, *Waranbegusa kenkyū* (Tokyo: Kazama shobō, 1973), p. 47.

[32]Senzai is a minor role in *Okina sanbasō* and is performed by either a noh or kyōgen actor
depending upon the school of noh with which it is performed. (In the noh schools known as
kamigakari — Kanze, Hosho, and Umewaka — a noh actor takes the Senzai role; in the
shimogakari schools — Komparu, Kongō, and Kita — a kyōgen actor performs Senzai.)

[33]Yonekura, *Waranbegusa kenkyū*, pp. 45-46.

[34]Furukawa Hisashi et al., eds., *Kyōgen jiten jikōhen*, pp. 20-22.

[35]Ikeda Hiroshi, *Kokyōgen daihon no hattatsu ni kanshiteno shoshiteki kenkyū* (Tokyo:
Kazama shobō, 1967), pp. 143-262. Contains a comparison of *Toraaki bon* and *Tenri bon*.

[36]Ibid., pp. 354-355.

[37]Ibid., pp. 372-378.

[38]See Furukawa Hisashi et al., eds., *Kyōgen jiten jikōhen* for a more detailed account.

THE SHAPING OF THE TEXT: *THE CRAB* : (pp. 41-54)

[1]Koyama Hiroshi et al., eds., *Noh kyōgen: kyōgen kanshō annai*, vol. 7 (Tokyo: Iwanami
shoten, 1990), p. 285.

[2]Furukawa Hisashi, ed., *Kyōgen kohon nishū* (Tokyo: Wanya shoten, 1968), p. 22.

[3]William LaFleur, *The Karma of Words* (Berkeley: University of California Press, 1983), pp.
141-142.

[4]Furukawa, *Kyōgen kohon nishū*, p. 23.

[5]Ibid., p. 23.

[6]Ikeda Hiroshi et al., *Ōkura Toraaki bon: kyōgen shū no kenkyū*, vol. 1 (Tokyo: Hyō-gensha, 1972), p. 427.

[7]Ikeda Hiroshi, *Kokyōgen daihon no hattatsu ni kanshiteno shoshiteki kenkyū* (Tokyo: Kazama shoten, 1967), p. 228.

[8]Ibid., p. 167.

[9]Ibid., pp. 165-166.

[10]In *Zoku kyōgenki* (1700), the crab actually sings the notes of the flute passage. This would support the thesis that this text was used basically by amateur groups as they would have been less likely to be able to afford to have musicians on stage. See *Kyōgen zenshū* (Tokyo: Kokuminbunko kankōkai, 1914), p. 365.

[11]See my translation of *The Crab* (from the *Kumogata bon* text).

[12]Sasano Ken, ed., *Noh kyōgen: Ōkura Torahiro bon*, vol. 2 (Tokyo: Iwanami bunko, 1977), p. 475. Kōshū is another name for Ōmi, the area around Lake Biwa.

[13]Ōkura Toraaki, "Waranbegusa," in Nishio Minoru et al., eds., *Yōkyoku kyōgen*, Kokugo kokubungaku kenkyūshi taisei, vol. 8 (Tokyo: Sanseidō, 1961), pp. 518.

[14]The complex relationship between folk tales and kyōgen is explored more fully in *Kyōgen ronkō* by Taguchi Kazuo, and in *Gekokujō no bungaku* by Satake Akihiro. Neither states unequivocally which came first, the tale or the play. Rather, the relationship seems to have been an ongoing one in which the influence went in both directions. In some plays, such as *Persimmons*, the relationship to tales and legends is evident as early as the *Tenshō bon* text. My point here is that the place name is included at a later date in *The Crab* in an effort to reestablish a connection with tale literature. See also, Koyama Hiroshi, ed., *Noh kyōgen: kyō gen no sekai*, vol. 5, pp. 249-264.

[15]Koyama Hiroshi et al., eds., *Noh kyōgen: kyōgen kanshō annai*, vol. 7, p. 285.

[16]Ikeda Hiroshi et al., eds., *Kyōgen*, vol. 4, Nihon shomin bunka shiryō shūsei (Tokyo: Sanichi Shobō, 1975), p. 332.

[17]In this context it is interesting to cite the play *Mamako* (Stepchild), which appears for the first time in the *Toraaki bon* text as a mountain priest play. *Mamako* is unusual in kyōgen because of its heavy Confucian moral tone and lack of humor. It was deleted from the Ōkura school texts after *Toraaki bon*. A stepmother is so jealous of her husband's attentions to her stepchild that she has a mountain priest come and cast a spell to kill the boy. She reports the death to her husband who summons the boy's mentor, a mountain priest from Mount Haguro, who brings him back to life. The mother is left alone onstage and exits with a sneeze. The sneeze ending, common in the "blindman plays," emphasizes her loneliness. The play was recast later, in mid-Edo, by the Izumi school, under the order of the Maeda daimyō of Kaga. The later play, *Mamako yamabushi*, is even more moralizing in tone. It is still a part of the Izumi school repertory although it has not been performed in recent times. Its appeal to the sensibilities of the ruling elite is clear.

[18]Sasano, *Noh kyōgen: Ōkura Torahiro bon*, vol. 2, p. 477.

[19]The passage from the *Torahiro bon* text quoted above is also found, for example, in the

Toraaki bon text for *Inu yamabushi* (Dog and the Mountain Priest) but without the exchange between the mountain priest and the secondary characters.

[20]Ikeda Hiroshi et al., eds., *Ōkura Toraaki bon: Kyōgenshū no kenkyū,* vol. 1, p. 428.

[21]Arthur Waley, *The Nō Plays of Japan* (New York: Grove, 1965), p. 188.

[22]Ibid.

[23]Ibid., p. 189.

[24] Ikeda Hiroshi, ed.,*Ōkura Toraaki bon: kyōgenshū no kenkyū,* vol. 1, p. 404.

[25]Ibid.

[26]Yokomichi Mario, ed., *Yōkyokushū,* vol. 2 , Nihon koten bungaku taikei, vol. 41 (Tokyo: Iwanami Shoten, 1980.) p. 175.

[27]Sasano, *Noh kyōgen: Ōkura Torahiro bon,* vol. 1, p. 477.

[28]Yokomichi, ed., *Yōkyokushū,* vol. 2, p. 169.

[29]Koyama Hiroshi, ed., *Noh kyōgen,* vol. 5, p. 65.

[30]Koyama Hiroshi, "Kyōgen no kotei," *Bungaku,* 16 (July 1948), p. 26.

[31]Koyama Hiroshi, ed., *Noh kyōgen,* vol. 5, pp. 298-301. Koyama discusses the use of kyōgen parody (*modoki*) in early texts. For example, the noh plays *Saigyō zakura* and *Ōshi,* both celebrating cherry blossoms, were originally followed by a kyōgen parody, *Hana ori.* In the noh plays the visual center of the stage is a spray of cherry blossoms. In early Edo the cherry blossom spray was left on stage for the kyōgen play which followed. During the course of the kyōgen play, the branches of the cherry are broken off. This was a clear parody of noh and not permitted in later years.

[32]In the *Lady Aoi* play, the *waki* (secondary) role is that of a mountain ascetic who has been summoned by the court to the bedside of Lady Aoi. The aikyōgen performs the role of messenger from the court. He approaches the hashigakari and stops at the first pine where he calls toward the curtain, "May I come in?" The *waki* appears in formal mountain priest dress which, unlike the kyōgen dress, includes wide, stiff, white trousers (*ōguchi*). He chants as he proceeds down the bridgeway,

> Before the window of the nine realms of the senses;
> On a pallet of the ten vehicles of the law;
> Sprinkled with the holy waters of yoga;
> Purified by the moon of the three mysteries;
> Who is it that seeks admittance here?
> (Arthur Waley, *The Nō Plays of Japan,* p. 187.)

In the kyōgen versions a farmer is, in one case, seeking the mountain priest's aid in ridding his garden of toadstools and, in another, in freeing his brother of a possessing owl spirit. The scene is parallel to that in the noh play except for the end of the chant of the mountain priest. In the kyōgen, the original is broken in the last line and the mountain priest drops the formal chanting rhythm and calls out, "Who's there?" (*ta so*).

[33]See my translation of *Mushrooms,* taken from the *Kotenbunko bon* text of the *Kumogata bon.*

THE MAN WITHIN THE MYTH: (pp. 55-78)

[1]Taguchi Kazuo, *Kyōgen ronkō* (Tokyo: Miyai shoten, 1977), p. 91.

[2]Ibid., p. 96; for an excellent translation of the tale (*Uji shūi monogatari* 2/14), see Royall Tyler, *Japanese Tales* (New York: Pantheon, 1987), p. 172.

[3]Andō Tsunejirō et al., *Kyōgen sōran* (Tokyo: Nōgaku shōrin, 1973), p. 3.

[4] Murayama Shūichi, *Yamabushi no rekishi* (Tokyo: Hanawa shobō, 1979), p. 306.

[5]Ibid.

[6]Honda Yasuji, *Yamabushi kagura, bangaku* (Tokyo: Iba shoten, 1971). See also, Ikeda Hiroshi et al., eds., *Kyōgen*, Nihon shomin bunka shiryō shūsei, vol. 4 (Tokyo: Sanichi shobō, 1975), p. 730; and Murayama Shūichi, *Yamabushi no rekishi*, pp. 329-345.

[7]H. Byron Earhart, *A Religious Study of the Mount Haguro Sect of Shugendō* (Tokyo: Sophia University Press, 1970).

[8]Murayama, *Yamabushi no rekishi*, p. 194.

[9]Ibid., pp. 291-315.

[10]Wakamori Tarō, *Wakamori Tarō chosakushū*, vol. 2 (Tokyo: Kōbundō, 1980), pp. 100-101.

[11]Donald Keene, *Anthology of Japanese Literature* (Rutland, Vermont: Tuttle, 1956), pp. 145-146.

[12]Edwin O. Reischauer, "The Izayoi Nikki," *Harvard Journal of Asiatic Studies*, 10:3-4 (1947), p. 340.

[13]The above information on the symbolism of the mountains is found in Carmen Blacker, *The Catalpa Bow* (London: George Allen and Unwin, 1975), p. 211.

[14]See Royall Tyler, *Japanese Tales*, pp. 127-130 ("The Wizard of the Mountains"), for a tale about En no gyōja from the *Nara ehon* giving details of his life. Other sources are the *Konjaku monogatari* and the *Nihon ryōiki*.

[15]"The Valley Rite" (*Tanikō*), translated by Royall Tyler in Donald Keene, *20 Plays of the Nō Theater* (New York: Columbia University Press, 1970), pp. 316-330.

[16]According to the *Nara ehon* version of the En no gyōja story, the Great Ascetic En summoned a god to Golden Peak (said to be a part of vulture Peak in India where the Buddha preached the Lotus Sutra) to save deluded beings. The god called forth was Zao Gongen. (See Tyler, *Japanese Tales*, p. 128.)

[17]Blacker, *The Catalpa Bow*, pp. 96-97.

[18]Ibid, p. 90.

[19]Ibid.

[20]Satake Akihiro, *Gekokujō no bungaku* (Tokyo: Chikuma shobō, 1982), p. 156.

[21]Wakamori, *Wakamori Tarō chosakushū*, p. 110.

[22]Blacker, *The Catalpa Bow*, pp. 95-97.

[23]Ikeda Hiroshi et al., eds., *Ōkura Toraaki bon: Kyōgenshū no kenkyū*, vol. 1 (Tokyo: Hyō gensha, 1972), pp. 420-421.

[24]Yokomichi Mario, ed., *Yōkyokushū*, vol. 2, Nihon koten bungaku taikei (Tokyo: Iwanami shoten, 1980), p. 175.

[25]See my translation, *Owls*.

[26]D. E. Mills, *A Collection of Tales from Uji* (Cambridge: Cambridge University Press, 1970), pp. 141-142.

[27]Ibid., pp. 142-143.

[28]Tyler, *Japanese Tales,* pp. 131-132.

[29]Satake, *Gekokujō no bungaku,* pp. 169-181.

[30]Yokomichi, ed., *Yōkyokushū,* vol. 2, pp. 69-78.

[31]Ibid., p. 72.

[32]Ibid., p. 72.

[33]Ibid., p. 76.

[34]Ibid., pp. 74-75.

[35]Ibid., pp. 74-75.

[36]Ibid., p. 75.

[37]Ikeda Hiroshi et al., eds.,*Ōkura Toraaki bon,* vol. 1, p. 429.

[38]Ibid., p. 430.

[39]See my translations, *Persimmons.*

[40]Tyler, *Japanese Tales,* pp. 130-131.

[41]The theme of the celebration of cleverness and the ridicule of naivety and innocence is important in European tales as well, as Robert Darnton points out in *The Great Cat Massacre* (New York: Random House, 1984.)

[42]Yokomichi Mario, ed., *Yōkyokushū,* vol. 1, p. 312.

[43]See my translations, *Persimmons.*

[44]See my translations, *Persimmons.*

[45]Satake, *Gekokujō no bungaku,* p. 137.

[46]See my translations, *Persimmons.*

[47]See *Persimmons.*

CONCLUSION: (pp. 79-81)

[1]Aoki Shinji, *Kyōgen men raisan* (Tokyo: Moga shoten, 1981), p. 158. Kobayashi Seki comments during the interview, "As for the kyōgen actor, even when he dons a mask, Nomura Manzō is still Nomura Manzō . . . that is, the Manzō expression shows through the mask." See also, Nomura Mansaku, "Some Thoughts on the Kyōgen Mask," in *Mime Journal: Nō/Kyōgen Masks and Performance* (Claremont, California: Pomona College Theater Department, 1984), pp. 177-183.

THE CRAB: (pp. 87-98)

[1] A translation of the play *Kaniyamabushi.* Performed by all schools. In the *Tenshō bon* the title appears as *Kanibakemono* (The Crab Spirit)

[2][Notes to the Actor: Alternate dress for the mountain priest consists of broad hakama and a three-quarter length travel cloak of silk or gauze.]

[3]The travel chest (*katabako*) is like that used in the noh play *Ataka.* Formerly a cedar hat and lunchbox were also attached to the staff. The size of the chest is approximately ten inches by

six and one-half inches.

[4][Notes to the Actor: A crab mask is worn by our school only. This mask may also be used for *Kaminari* (Thunder God).] Currently the *kentoku* mask is used by most schools.

[5] In contemporary performances there is no musical accompaniment.

[6][Notes to the Actor: The mountain priest carries a staff over his right shoulder with a cedar hat attached. Or, he may carry it in his left hand. The porter marches with legs high as well.]

[7][Notes to the Actor: The porter brags and blusters foolishly. When he says, "with my stick" he should look up at the staff and remove the hat which he flings upstage toward the stagehand. When he loses his grip on the staff, he staggers about in front of the crab.]

[8]Irataka beads are power beads used by the mountain priests when performing incantations or exorcisms. They are made from a collection of animal bones and teeth, etc.

[9]*Boron:* Often appears in mountain priest incantations in kyōgen and appears to be a reduction of the mantra to the universal Buddha (Dainichi Nyorai).

[10]A Buddhist version of a children's ABC song said to have been compiled in the eighth century by Kūkai.

[11][Notes to the Actor: In the past the shagiri flute ending was used. However, that is out of date. Today the actor should decide for himself how best to please his audience.]

THE LUNCHBOX THIEF: (pp. 99-108)

[1]Translation of *Tsuto yamabushi.* Performed by all schools of kyōgen. The title appears as *Tsutokai* in the *Tenshō bon.* The play does not appear in the Sagi or Ōkura school texts until late Edo and Meiji, respectively. An alternative title appears in some of the Izumi school texts: *Miyage yamabushi.*

[2][Notes to the Actor: The prayer beads are chinaberry beads which he calls irataka beads. If the actor happens to possess irataka beads, they can be used instead. It is simply that by calling the chinaberry beads irataka beads you get a comic effect.]

[3][Notes to the Actor: In some early texts the lunch thief is the shite.]

[4][Notes to the Actor: Each character enters separately, introduces himself, and then falls asleep: first, the woodcutter, then the mountain priest, and after a short interval, the thief. The intervals between entrances should vary in length. The actor can try out different lengths but in any case the intervals should not be exactly the same.]

[5][Notes to the Actor: When the woodcutter moves in his sleep, the thief is startled and stands up. Just as he's wondering what to do next, the woodcutter falls back to sleep. The thief laughs, relieved.]

[6][Notes to the Actor: The thief should thrust the lunchbox behind the priest's head so that the woodcutter won't have it in his immediate view.

Alternative:

> a) Thief: Now then, to eat. (*Carries lunchbox to the stagehand spot and eats with his back to the audience. He returns with the lunchbox to the shite spot.*) That was very tasty. I'm full to bursting! I'll catch a few winks myself.
>
> But what if they open their eyes and accuse me of stealing? That'd be terrible.

What'll I do? I know! I'll slide the lunchbox over by the mountain priest so
it'll look like he ate it. (The above staging is fine. Or, you can stick a grain of rice on the
mountain priest's cheek but that's really vulgar.)

> b) Thief: That was close! Now I'll get down to eating. (*Begins to gobble up the
> lunch so fast that he starts to choke and rolls his eyes. He rubs his chest until he
> can swallow. You can perform a variety of such amusing actions during this
> scene.*]

7[Notes to the Actor: The stagehand removes the pole, scythe, and lunchbox at this juncture.]

8Fudō Myōō: Guardian deity of the mountain priests. He carries a rope in his left hand to catch
evil beings.

9[Notes to the Actor: If the bridgeway is long the thief may stop at the shite spot and call out,
"Please! Stop!"]

10From a Kamakura period children's song. Only one verse appears here. (See Furukawa
Hisashi et al., eds., *Kyōgen jiten goihen* (Tokyo: Tokyodō, 1963), p. 342.) In the *Tenshō bon*
text this song is followed by a children's counting song also popular at the time, called
Zorikeri. Satake Akihiro argues that the songs were taken up by the kyōgen actors to parody
the mountain priest in *Gekokujō no Bungaku* (Tokyo: Chikuma shobō, 1982), p. 140.

11He passes in front of the thief and performs a *hiraki* (thrusts chest forward with arms held at
the side) at the first pine on the bridgeway.

12[Notes to the Actor: No matter how long or short the bridgeway, the mountain priest prays
twice, rubbing his beads. He should change places with the woodcutter and move downstage.
It is standard for the mountain priest to face the thief as he prays.]

13[Notes to the Actor:

> alternative endings:

> a. Staggering, the thief wobbles off stage chased by the priest. From "Don't wish
> you hadn't later, man!" the mountain priest faces the thief and declaims. He
> forms a mudra and claps his hands, pointing in the direction first of the thief and
> then of the woodcutter. He continues praying, facing front. From "I offer a
> prayer," he stops rubbing the beads. Then he faces the woodcutter and starts
> rubbing the beads and chanting, "Boron, boron, boron. . ."

> b. Though he prays at the woodcutter, there is no reaction. He then turns again to
> the lunch thief and prays. The atmosphere grows eerie. When the thief   tries to
> head toward the bridgeway, the woodcutter orders him to stay and seizes hold of
> him. The priest follows them, praying more and more intently in the direction of
> the thief. The thief is prayed to a halt at the first pine on the bridgeway. He acts
> as if he's paralyzed. The woodcutter is shocked, and suddenly lets go of him.
> Whereupon the thief falls on his seat, much to the woodcutter's disgust. The
> paralyzed thief now calls out, "I'm wretched! Please! Stop!" while the mountain
> priest begins "irises under the bridge." The thief becomes more and more
> uncomfortable. He is prayed backward and staggers until he falls on one knee at
> the shite spot. The woodcutter is on the   right side of the mountain priest. From

here the mountain priest continues to pray, "boron, boron, boron" and to rub the beads.

    c. The priest prays the lunch thief to a standstill and then draws him back to center stage where the thief plops down on his seat in pain. The mountain priest announces, "You've been found out!" The woodcutter grabs the thief's right wrist. Various actions may accompany the scene in which the woodcutter leads the mountain priest off stage. For example, the thief may continue to cry, "It hurts! It hurts!" until they have exited. Watching them exit, he may stagger to a standing position and call after them. Or he may follow them as far as the shite spot and, clinging to the pillar, cry, "It still hurts!" and then wobble to center stage where his hands and feet freeze and he falls on his seat. He then pulls himself up and exits. Or he may wobble off stage. If the bridgeway is long, you may have to think of an appropriate exit. If it is short, you can simply stagger off.

    d. When he sees the woodcutter leading the mountain priest off, the thief cries, "Oh, I'm wretched!" When he is prayed backward, he cries "Help me! Please help me!" He may raise his hands together pleadingly and so forth. He may also be pulled backward by the prayer and wobble off backward.

    e. In former times, there was a shagiri flute ending. This is no longer used.]

MUSHROOMS: (pp. 109-121)

[1] A translation of the play *Kusabira*. This play is performed by both the Izumi and Ōkura schools and was also part of the repertory for the now defunct Sagi school (see *Sagi Deneimon Yasunori bon*, 1704 - 1715). It is not found in the *Tenshō bon* (1570).

[2] [Notes to the Actor:

    1. All mushrooms are masked and their bodies should be devoid of expression. Expression is in the hats. The mushrooms should pick a spot and crouch there with their backs erect. When they enter and leave the stage, they should maintain their posture, bending only from the knees and walking in a squatting position.

    2. When there are more mushrooms than masks, scarves may be used instead.

    3. All mushrooms tuck their hands into their sleeves and clutch them to their chest or fold them over their chest. (Demon mushroom is the exception.)]

[3] *Reishi*, also known as the ten-thousand-year mushroom (*mannen take*) and therefore a probable symbol of longevity.

[4] Masks: Only the princess mushroom and the demon mushroom are assigned specific masks. The others may wear the *kentoku* mask (pop eyes, prominent teeth), the *usobuki* mask (pop eyes and a pursed mouth), or the *noborihige* mask (flat nose, wrinkles, and a beard).

[5] [Note to the Actor: The mushrooms should shuffle onstage without wobbling. Crouch but keep your back erect and clutch your sleeves to your chest.]

[6] [Note to the Actor: If the bridgeway is short, then you may start reciting from the curtain. Otherwise, use your own discretion.]

[7] Taken from the noh play *Aoi no Ue* (see Yokomichi Mario, ed., *Yōkyokushū* vol.1, Nihon koten bungaku taikei, vol. 40 (Tokyo: Iwanami shoten, 1980), p. 129.) where it is recited by a

powerful ascetic. The following meeting of the neighbor and the mountain priest is a parody of the meeting between the aikyōgen messenger from the court and the ascetic in the noh play.

[Notes to the Actor: The copying of the *Aoi no ue* greeting scene is not a traditional device. It seems to have been a sudden inspiration. However, this parody is now an accepted technique. Since it is rather discourteous to the noh waki (the actor performing the ascetic in *Aoi no ue*), the dynamic mode of chanting may be omitted.]

[8]This is a parody of the mountain priest incantation recited by Benkei in the noh play *Ataka* (Yokomichi, ed., *Yōkyokushū*, vol. 2, p. 175) which begins, "A mountain priest is one who follows in the path of the Great Ascetic En and models himself after the visage of the guardian king Fudō. / A tokin represents the crown of the five wisdoms and is pleated in the twelve karmic ties and worn on the head....

[9]Irataka beads are power beads used by the mountain priest when performing incantations or exorcisms. They are made from a collection of animal bone and teeth, etc.

[10]A Kamakura period children's song, sometimes followed by a children's counting song. Children's songs are presumably used to parody the mountain priest.

[11]*Fudō Myōō*, the guardian deity of the mountain priest. He is one of the fierce bright kings who protect the Buddha, Dainichi Nyorai.

[12][Note to the Actor: Make up some mudra for the eggplant. It's best done surreptitiously.]

[13][Note to the Actor:

> a. This ending is very important and should be timed and performed carefully.
>
> b. Alternative ending: The demon mushroom is not used. When the neighbor is chased off stage, half of the mushrooms remain on stage as follows:
>
> Priest: This won't do. He's fled. Oh no! This is terrible. Now I'll pray the (*They all begin to quiver and he is left standing in the middle of them. Revolted, he makes the eggplant sign.*)
>
> Boron, boron. . .
>
> (*He prays and heads for the shite pillar as he makes the eggplant sign. The mushrooms follow him.*)
>
> Boron, boron. . .
>
> (*Prays over and over again but finally stops when he reaches the first pine.*) I can't bear it! Get away from me! (*Flees with the silent mushrooms in pursuit.*)
>
> c. In the old days the play ended on a shagiri flute melody and there were other alternate endings but that was the old style. I'm not at all sure how they would go over today.]

OWLS: (pp. 123-131)

[1]Translation of the play *Fukurō yamabushi*. Found in all schools of kyōgen and in the *Tenshō bon*.

[Notes to the Actor: The entire play is a parody of the noh play *Aoi no ue* and should be performed as such but in an appealing manner.]

[2][Notes to the Actor: The mountain priest may wear an alternative costume resembling that of

the noh mountain priest but it must be in kyōgen style.]

3[Notes to the Actor: He may also come out with one leg of the hakama tied and one loose, but if it's too twisted it isn't interesting.]

4[Notes to the Actor: If the bridgeway is short, start chanting from the curtain. Otherwise, use your own judgment.]

5[Notes to the Actor: Up to "I go nowhere," he sings in noh style in parody of the waki mountain priest role in the noh play *Aoi no ue*. He then continues in normal kyōgen voice. It shouldn't be a serious parody of the noh. Whereas the waki mountain priest appears very dignified and grand, the kyōgen priest should exaggerate his weak points and appear self-important and ridiculous.]

6[Notes to the Actor: From the start Tarō looks ill. His head droops and he is in a daze. From time to time he draws his arms and legs together as if in pain. He yawns and flaps his arms like wings.]

7Taken from the noh play *Aoi no ue*, where it is recited by a powerful ascetic to free Lady Aoi of the possessing spirit of Lady Rokujō.

8[Notes to the Actor: The actor must make up a sign.]

9[Notes to the Actor: When the priest claps his hands, Tarō should look startled and writhe in pain.]

10[Notes to the Actor: The three exit separately with individual gestures. It is a good technique to have them flap their arms like wings. The exit should not be drawn out too long. The three should continue to hoot at each other until they've exited.]

[Notes to the Actor: Alternative endings:

  a. The three collide and topple over. Tarō and his brother exit hooting and staggering. The mountain priest staggers upright and recovers his senses before exiting.

  b. The three collide and topple over. All three hoot together and then recover their senses and exit, the mountain priest first, followed by Tarō and his brother.

  c. In the old days a shagiri flute ending was used but this is old fashioned.

  d. In the Ōkura school texts the mountain priest exits crying, *nori suri oke* (literally, "leave the paste"). This is a line from a poem composed by Saigyō. "Behind the fields of Mount Shibumi / The owls cry, 'nori suri oke.'" (Apparently the birds liked to eat the paste prepared for gluing paper doors. It is the subject of a fairy tale, *Shita kiri suzume*, in which sparrows eat up an old woman's paste.) According to the *Ise sangū meisho zue*, Saigyō is referring to the many owls in the remains of the castle of Fujimasa of Shibumi Otobe Hyōgo in Tsu province.]

PERSIMMONS: (pp. 133-145)

1A translation of *Kakiyamabushi*. Found in all schools of kyōgen. In the *Tenshō bon* collection, the title appears as *Kakikui yamabushi*.

2In modern performances there is no musical accompaniment.

3"kai wo mo motanu yamabushi wa kai wo mo motanu yamabushi wa michi, michi uso wo fukō yo."

The mountain priest carried a conch shell (*kai*) as part of his equipment. A pun is intended on the word "kai" which can also mean "commandments." A second pun occurs in the final line "uso wo fuku" which has the alternative meaning of "to whistle."

[Notes to the Actor: The last line is picked up by the chorus as a refrain. The stagehand may substitute for the chorus if the shidai is sung without musical accompaniment. Or, the actor himself may take up the refrain softly. However, this is not a successful technique. The actor must work it out for himself.]

[4][Notes to the actor: This time one circular sweep is enough.]

[5][Notes to the actor: The actor must mime eating without holding onto the pillar. He picks a persimmon by stretching out his arm and plucking. He should employ various odd movements. It is good technique to eat with both hands. He should look as if he is taking the persimmons up in his hands and biting into them. For the juicy ones, he should suck on them. In order to climb the tree, a *kazuraoke* (lacquer tub) should be placed near the waki pillar. Although he may stand on this and eat, it is not as amusing as standing on the railing.]

[6][Notes to the Actor: The owner turns to the shite spot and performs a hiraki.]

[7]Based on an incantation from the noh play *Dampū*, where it is used by a mountain priest to pray a boat back into port.

[8]A Kamakura period children's song.

[9][Notes to the Actor: stagger in time to the rhythm of the incantation and fall at the priest's feet.]

[10][Notes to the Actor: When the mountain priest is played by a child, the play ends with the owner carrying him off.]

SACROILIAC: (pp. 147-160)

[1]A translation of the play *Koshi inori*. Found in all texts of all schools. In the *Tenshō bon* only the title remains, *Inori goshi*.

[2]A Buddhist version of a children's ABC song from the eighth century; popularly attributed to Kūkai.

[3] [Notes to the Actor: Grandfather is bent over backward and should look extremely uncomfortable.]

[4][Notes to the Actor: At first he should appear to pray softly but then, forgetting himself, he should get louder and louder.]

[5][Notes to the Actor: In early Edo texts a *shagiri* flute ending was used.]

THE SHINTO PRIEST AND THE MOUNTAIN PRIEST: (pp. 161-177)

[1]Translation of *Negi yamabushi*. Found in all schools and texts of kyōgen. A similar play, *Inu yamabushi* (The Dog and the Mountain Priest), is also found in the *Kotenbunko bon* version of the text but with large sections deleted where they are the same as in *The Shinto Priest Meets the Mountain Priest*. The main difference between the two is that a dog instead of a daikoku

statue is the object of the prayer contest between the Shinto and mountain priests. *The Dog and the Mountain Priest* is not found in the *Tenshō bon*, nor in any other text after the Meiji period.

[2]Daikoku is one of the seven household gods of good fortune.

[3][Notes to the Actor: In the past burlap shoes were worn but these have been eliminated.]

[4]Entrance music is not included in current performances.

[5][Notes to the Actor: A lid from a kazuraoke barrel may be used instead. In the old days, the lid was used. The stagehand places the kazuraoke barrel seat in front of the musicians spot during the Shinto priest's travel scene.]

[6][Notes to the Actor: The tea dealer takes the cup up in his right hand and moves it from his left side to directly in front of him. Opening his fan he dips and pours the tea into the cup. To pour from a kettle is unesthetic. It is best to pour directly into the cup. Even when cooling the tea, it is better to pour it directly from the fan to the cup. The actor should place the open fan to his right and take up the cup in his right hand. He then passes the cup to his left hand and offers it to the priest. The priest moves his prayer wand from his right shoulder to his left. After drinking the tea, he restores the wand to his right shoulder. The tea dealer takes the cup in his left hand, wipes it clean, and places it to his left. He then closes his fan and tucks it into his belt. The priest should remain seated.]

[7]In modern performances there is no chorus onstage and the refrain is taken up either by the stagehand or by the mountain priest himself in a softer voice.

[8]Ōmine and Kazuragi were two of the holy peaks where mountain priests performed austerities.

[9]4 a.m.

[10] The travel case (*katabako*) contains sutras and other Buddhist implements.

[11][Notes to the Actor: If he has taken out his fan, he must tuck it away again after he puts down the travel case.]

[12]*Gyōriki tsure*, an acolyte who accompanies a mountain priest and carries his chest for him.

[13]*Daikoku ten*, one of the seven Shinto gods of good fortune; dressed in a beret and carrying a purse over the left shoulder and a hammer in the right hand.

[14][Notes to the Actor: (alternative text) What? You're talking nonsense. We pray to any number of gods but we've never prayed to anything so mediocre as a daikoku before.]

[15][Notes to the Actor: The Shinto priest circles the inner area of the stage past the shite spot. He tries to sneak off toward the bridgeway but the mountain priest catches sight of him and shakes his right fist, angrily. The frightened Shinto priest resumes his former position, with the mountain priest watching him. The mountain priest then faces front and lowers his fist in a dignified manner. The Shinto priest watches him and then performs a hiraki. Then, glancing at the mountain priest, he circles the stage in an outer circle (left to right), proceeding stealthily. The mountain priest spots him and leaps into the air coming down on his left knee with his right leg extended forward. With a fierce look, he grasps his sword hilt and wraps his beads around his wrist. The Shinto priest drops to one knee in alarm. Quietly, he circles back to his former postition on-stage. The mountain priest keeps an eye on him and then stands and

performs a hiraki. Passing his beads to his left hand, he holds them as before and faces front.]

[16][Notes to the Actor: The daikoku must maintain an erect torso while bending from the knees in a crouch. He should shuffle across the stage without rocking his torso.]

[17]The following prayer is recited by Shinto priests while performing a kagura dance. It appears in the Noh play *Miwa*.

[18]Isuzugawa is the clear stream running through the precincts of the Grand Shrine at Ise.

[19][Notes to the Actor: When he comes to 'Bestow thy mercy upon me," he turns to face the daikoku and, taking the wand in his right hand, waves it. He asks for a blessing with both hands together and then, shaking the wand up and down, repeats, "I pray to thee, again and again," dancing from foot to foot in time to the beat. During the prayer the mountain priest should look as if he can't resist watching. At first he restrains himself, but finally he starts glancing around in a comical manner. He begins to listen to the priest's prayer from "humbly I beseech thee."]

[20][Notes to the Actor: When the tea dealer declares "a miracle!" the Shinto priest stops dancing and holding the wand at his side he peers over at the Mountain Priest. He then replaces the wand on his shoulder and returns to his earlier spot.]

[21]The incantation is a parody of that found in the noh play *Ataka*:

> A mountain priest is one who follows in the steps of the Great Ascetic En,
> the very living incarnation of the Guardian King Fudō.
> A tokin is the crown of five wisdoms,
> pleated into the twelve karmic links of rebirth;
> the persimmon-colored suzukake are the nine-layered diamond mandala;
> the black leggings are the black of the womb mandala;
> treading the eight-holed straw sandals, we tread the eight-petaled lotus.
> Breathing out, breathing in, we intone "Ah" and "Un."
> The mountain priest is a living Buddha, in this very body.

[22][Notes to the Actor: No matter how hard the mountain priest prays, the daikoku won't budge. Finally, he grabs the daikoku's sleeve which results in the daikoku whacking him over the head with his hammer. The mountain priest backs off, praying, and the daikoku spins around to face the Shinto priest. The Tea dealer's exclamation, "Well! This is altogether different!" occurs when the daikoku first turns back to the Shinto priest. The mountain priest looks offended and prays even louder. The tea dealer faces front to speak but then moves out of the way when the daikoku strikes the mountain priest.]

[23][Notes to the Actor: The mountain priest may perform a mudra.]

[24][Notes to the Actor: The daikoku knocks the mountain priest over somewhere between the third and fifth "boron." When the Shinto priest repeats "I pray to thee, again and again," the daikoku becomes quite elated and dances around from foot to foot, following
the Shinto priest. Each time the mountain priest tries to turn him around, he strikes him with his mallet and turns back to the Shinto priest.]

[25][Notes to the Actor:

Alternative endings:

a. When the mountain priest steps back and prays, the daikoku chases him with the mallet as far as the shite spot. The mountain priest cries out, "Let me go, let me go!" and finally flees off stage with his beads dangling from his right hand. The tea dealer picks up the chest in both hands and exits, followed by the Shinto priest.

b. Tea Dealer	Well, well! We've got a winner! Well, well, we've got a winner!
Shinto Priest	Carry it! Carry it!
Mountain Priest	Tea Dealer! Get him off of me!
Tea dealer	You must carry it! You must carry it!
Mountain priest	Get away from me! Get away from me!
Shinto Priest	Take it! Take it!
Mountain Priest	Please let me go! Let me go!
Tea dealer	Take it! Take it!]

THE SNAIL: (pp. 179-194)

[1] A translation of the play *Kagyū*. This play is found in the Izumi and Sagi texts but not in the Okura texts until the Meiji period. It is not found in the *Tenshō bon*.

[2] [Notes to the Actor: When performed with noh, it is customary to have shidai opening music. The shidai, which is usually sung by the mountain priest, is the "three peaks" shidai.]

[3] 1 a.m..

[4] 4 a.m.

[5] [Notes to the Actor: (alternative text) I have an uncle over one hundred years old who claims that snails are medicine for longevity, so I'll call my son and send him out after one.]

[6] The snail song is a popular children's song dating back to medieval times. Various versions exist. The version below is from the *Ryōjin hishō* (translated by Arthur Waley in Donald Keene, *Anthology of Japanese Literature* (Rutland, Vt: Tuttle, 1956), p. 168).

> Dance, dance, Mr. Snail
> If you won't I shall leave you
> For the little horse
> For the little ox
> To tread under his hoof
> To trample to bits . . .

[7] [Notes to the Actor: When the mountain priest dances from foot to foot in time to the song, he doesn't need to keep lifting his legs high. However, he must maintain his mountain priest appearance somehow. His movements should be exaggerated, rapid, and rough, and should keep time with the beat. The mountain priest should appear delighted with the child's absorption in the rhythm. (He should of course resume the mountain priest walk in between dancing.)]

[8] [Notes to the Actor: When Tarō turns to the mountain priest, the priest should command, "sing, sing!"]

[9] [Notes to the Actor: After stamping to the right the mountain priest turns to the left and

performs a hiraki. He then rushes downstage center and stamps in time to the beat. He repeats, "Come out, come out! Snail, snail!" and goes to the waki spot where he turns around sharply to face center stage. He makes several small circles in time to the beat (from front center around to the waki spot and back). Tarō and the priest meet at stage center and head left together singing, "snail, snail-l-l!" However, Tarō stops singing, and when the priest notices him talking again with his father he tugs on Tarō's sleeve.]

[10]The mountain priest's chanting occurs simultaneously with the dialogue between the father and son which follows.

[11][Notes to the Actor: The mountain priest is hidden from those onstage but not from the audience. He quickly darts out to center stage without the father and Tarō observing. They continue to look for him in the same place. The father calls out, "Now where'd he go," and raises his fan to strike the priest. When they can't find him they are puzzled. They pass directly in front of him and the father proceeds to the waki spot while Tarō passes behind the priest. He then heads upstage until he faces the priest.]

GLOSSARY OF KYŌGEN TERMS

The terms defined below are only those which appear in the translations of the kyōgen plays. For a more complete glossary of noh terms see the glossary in Bethe and Brazell, *Dance in the Nō Theater*, vol. 3 (1982).

Ado	The secondary character or characters in a kyōgen play.
Aikyōgen	The kyōgen actor who appears within a noh play.
Chorus spot	The position at the left of the stage in front of the area where the chorus would sit in a noh play.
Dynamic mode	The noh singing style known as *tsuyogin* and characterized by the intensity of the voice rather than pitch. *Tsuyogin* is used in contrast to *yowagin* which is the melodic mode based on a tonal scale.
Hashigakari	The bridgeway onto a noh stage that connects the stage to the off-stage area behind a small curtain.
Hiraki	A movement borrowed from the noh in which the actor steps three steps backward while spreading his arms out to the sides. In kyōgen the *hiraki* usually indicates a change of mood in the character or scene.
Maibataraki	Danced action in a noh play accompanied by flute, and all three drums.
Michiyuki	A travel scene during which the kyōgen actor recites as he circles the stage.
Musicians spot	The postion at the rear of the stage in front of the area where the musicians would sit in a noh play.
Nanori	A name announcement scene during which the kyōgen actor introduces himself.
Nohgakari	Kyōgen plays that are based on the formal features of a noh play.

215

Pine trees   The three pines placed along the *hashigakari* to mark postions for the actors. The first pine is the pine closest to the stage.

Shidai   A passage of metered verse sung by the main kyōgen actor in the mountain priest, god, demon, and *nohgakari* plays after he has entered the stage.

Shite   The main actor in a kyōgen play.

Shite spot   The upstage right area of the stage. The *shite* actor performs the *nanori* at this spot.

Waki spot   The downstage left area of the noh stage where the secondary performer in a noh play, the waki, would normally sit.

Bibliography

ENGLISH SOURCES

Artaud, Antonin. *Antonin Artaud Collected Works.* Vol. 4. London, England: Calder and Boyers Ltd., 1964.

Bakhtin, Mikhail. *Rabelais and His World.* Bloomington, Indiana: Indiana University Press, 1984.

Bethe, Monica and Brazell, Karen. *Dance in the Noh Theater.* Vols.1-3. East Asia Papers, no. 29. Ithaca, New York: Cornell University , 1982.
____. *Nō as Performance: An Analysis of the Kuse Scene of Yamamba.* East Asia Papers, no. 16. Ithaca, New York: Cornell University, 1978.

Berberich, Junko Sakaba. "Rapture in Kyōgen." Ph.D. dissertation, University of Hawaii, 1982.

Blacker, Carmen. *The Catalpa Bow.* London: George Allen and Unwin, 1975.

Brandon, James. *Kabuki: Five Classic Plays.* Cambridge: Harvard University Press, 1975.
____. "Training at the Waseda Little Theater: The Suzuki Method." *The Drama Review* 22:4 (December 1978).

Brazell, Karen. *Twelve Plays of the Noh and Kyōgen Theaters.* East Asia Papers, no. 50. Ithaca, New York: Cornell University, 1988.

Brook, Peter. *The Empty Space.* New York: Antheneum, 1981.

Brower, Robert and Miner, Earl. *Japanese Court Poetry.* Stanford: Stanford University Press, 1961.

Chekov, Michael. *To The Actor.* New York: Harper and Row, 1953.

Darnton, Robert. *The Great Cat Massacre.* New York: Random House, 1985.

Earhart, Byron H. *A Religious Study of the Mount Haguro Sect of Shugendō.* Tokyo: Sophia University Press, 1970.

Esslin, Martin. *Reflections: Essays on Modern Theater.* New York: Doubleday Inc., 1969.
____. *Theater of the Absurd.* New York: Penguin Books, 1980.

Falk, R. P. *The Antic Muse.* New York: Grove Press, 1955.

Fenollosa, Ernst and Pound, Ezra. *Noh As Accomplishment.* London: MacMillan, 1916.

Frye, Northrop. *Anatomy of Criticism.* Princeton: Princeton University Press, 1973.

Goff, Janet. *Noh Drama and The Tale of Genji.* Princeton: Princeton University Press, 1991.

Golay, Jacqueline. "Pathos and Farce, Zatō Plays of the Kyōgen Repertoire." *Monumenta Nipponica* 28:2 (Summer 1973).

Grotwoski, Jerzy. *Towards a Poor Theater.* New York: Simon and Schuster, 1968.

Hall, John Whitney and Toyoda, Takeshi, eds. *Japan in the Muromachi Age.* Berkeley: University of California Press, 1977.

Haynes, Carolyn. "Parody in Kyōgen." *Monumenta Nipponica* 39 (1984).
____. "Parody in the Maikyōgen and the Monogurui Kyōgen." Ph.D. dissertation. Cornell University, January 1988.

Keene, Donald. *Twenty Plays of the Nō Theater.* New York: Columbia University Press, 1970.
____. *Anthology of Japanese Literature.* Rutland, Vermont: Tuttle, 1956.
____. *Nō: The Classical Theater of Japan.* Palo Alto, California: Kodansha International, 1966.
____. *The Battles of Coxinga.* Cambridge: CambridgeUniversity Press, 1971.
____. *World within Walls.* New York: Holt, Rinehart, Winston, 1976.

Keir, Elam. *The Semiotics of Theater and Drama*. London: Methuen, 1980.

Kenny, Don. *A Guide to Kyōgen*. Tokyo: Hinoki shoten, 1968.

LaFleur, William R. *The Karma of Words*. Berkeley: University of California Press, 1983.

Lauter, Paul. *Theories of Comedy*. New York: Doubleday, 1964.

McDonald, Gerald D. and Conway, Michael. *The Films of Charlie Chaplin*. New York: Bonanza Books, 1965.

McKeon, Richard. *The Basic Works of Aristotle*. New York: Random House, 1941.

McKinnon, Richard. *Selected Plays of Kyōgen*. Tokyo: Uniprint, 1968.

Mills, D. E. *A Collection of Tales From Uji*. Cambridge: Cambridge University Press, 1970.

Muecke, D. C. *Irony and the Ironic*. London: Methuen, 1970.

Nishikawa, Kyōtarō. *Bugaku Masks*. Translated by Monica Bethe. New York: Kodansha International, 1978.

Nomura, Mansaku. "Some Thoughts on the Kyōgen Mask." In *Mime Journal: Nō/Kyōgen Masks and Peformance*. Claremont, California: Pomona College Theater, 1984.

O'Neill, P. G. *Early Nō Drama*. London: Lund Humphries, 1958. Reprint Westport, Connecticut: Greenwood, 1974.

Reischauer, Edwin O. "The Izayoi Nikki," *Harvard Journal of Asiatic Studies* 10:3-4 (1947).

Rimer, J. Thomas and Yamazaki, Masakazu. *On the Art of the Nō Drama*. Princeton: Princeton University Press, 1984.

Sakanishi, Shio. *The Ink Smeared Lady*. Rutland, Vermont: Tuttle, 1961.

Sansom, George. *A History of Japan, 1334-1617.* Stanford: Stanford University Press, 1961.

Shibano, Dorothy. "Kyōgen: The Comic As Drama." Ph.D. dissertation, University of Washington, 1973.

Skord, Virginia. *Tales of Tears and Laughter.* Honolulu: University of Hawaii Press, 1991.

Southern, Richard. *The Seven Ages of the Theater.* New York: Hill and Wang, 1961.

Styan, J. L. *The Dark Comedy.* Cambridge: Cambridge University Press, 1966.

Swinburne, Charles. *The Comedies of William Shakespeare.* Oxford: Oxford University Press, 1961.

Sypher, Wylie. *Comedy.* Baltimore: Johns Hopkins University Press, 1956.

Turner, Victor. *The Ritual Process.* Ithaca, New York: Cornell University Press, 1966.
_____. *Dramas, Fields and Metaphors.* Ithaca, New York: Cornell University Press, 1974.

Tyler, Royall. *Japanese Tales.* New York: Pantheon, 1987.
_____. *Pining Wind: A Cycle of Nō Plays.* East Asia Papers, no.17. Ithaca, New York: Cornell University, 1980.
_____. *Granny Mountains: A Second Cycle of Nō Plays.* East Asia Papers, no.18. Ithaca, New York: Cornell University, 1980.

Ury, Marian. *Tales of Times Now Past.* Berkeley, California: University of California Press, 1979.

Veyne, Paul. *Did the Greeks Believe in Their Myths.* Chicago: University of Chicago Press, 1988.

Waley, Arthur. *The Nō Plays of Japan.* London: G. Allen and Unwin, 1921. Reprint New York: Grove Press, 1965.

Wilbur, Richard. *Moliere: The Misanthrope and Tartuffe.* New York: Harcourt Brace Jovanovich, 1965.

Willett, John, trans. *Brecht on Theater.* New York: Hill and Wang, 1971.

Wycherley, William. *The Country Wife.* New York: Random House, 1956.

JAPANESE SOURCES

Aoki Shinji. *Kyōgen men raisan.* Tokyo: Moga shoten, 1981.

Andō Tsunejirō et al. *Kyōgen sōran.* Tokyo: Nōgaku shorin, 1973.

Araki Yoshio and Shigeyama Sennojō. *Kyōgen.* Osaka: Sōgensha, 1956.

Furukawa Hisashi et al. *Kyōgen jiten jikōhen.* Tokyo: Tokyodō, 1976.
_____. *Kyōgen jiten goihen.* Tokyo: Tokyodō, 1963.
_____. *Kyōgen kohon nishū.* Tokyo: Wanya, 1968.
_____. *Kyōgen no sekai.* Tokyo: Shakai shisōsha, 1960.
_____. *Kyōgen no kenkyū.* Tokyo: Fukumura, 1948.
_____. *Kyōgen shū,* vols. 1, 2 Nihon koten zensho. Tokyo: Asahi shimbun, 1970.

Gotō Hajime. *Nōgaku no Kigen.* Tokyo: Mokujisha, 1976.

Harada Toshiaki and Takahashi Mitsugu. *Nihon ryōiki.* Tokyo: Heibonsha, 1976.

Hata Tōru. "Kyōgen no hayashigoto," in *Geinō no kagaku geinō ronkō,* vol. 5. Tokyo: Kitamura, 1979.
_____."Kyakuhon ron," in *Geinō no kagaku geinō ronkō,* vol. 2. Tokyo: Kitamura, 1977.

Hayashiya Tatsusaburo. *Chūsei bunka no kichō.* Tokyo: Iwanami shoten, 1973.
_____. *Chūsei geinōshi no kenkyū.* Tokyo: Iwanami shoten, 1976.
_____. "Chūsei geinō no shakaiteki kiban." *Bungaku* 16 (December 1948):707-715.
_____. "Kyōgen ni okeru warai." *Bungaku* 21 (August 1953):797-802.
_____. "Momoyama jidai igo no noh, kyōgen." *Kokubungaku: kaishaku to kanshō* 269 (October 1958):35-39.

Honda Yasuji. *Noh oyobi kyōgen kō.* Tokyo: Nōgaku shorin, 1980.
_____. *Okina sono hoka.* Tokyo: Myōzendō, 1958.
_____. *Yamabushi kagura, bangaku.* Tokyo: Iba shoten, 1976.

Ikeda Hiroshi. *Kokyōgen daihon no hattatsu ni kanshiteno shoshiteki kenkyū.* Tokyo: Kazama shobō, 1967.

_____. *Kyōgen: okashi no keifu*. Nihon koten geinō, vol. 4. Tokyo: Heibonsha, 1970.

_____. "Kyōgen shishō no sogen:'yamabushi no kyōgen' o chūshin to shite." *Kokugo to kokubungaku* (January 1957):46-57.

_____ et al., eds. *Ōkura Toraaki bon: kyōgenshū no kenkyū*, vols. 1, 2. Tokyo: Hyōgensha, 1972.

_____ et al., eds., *Kyōgen*. Nihon shomin bunka shiryō shūsei, vol. 4. Tokyo:Sanichi shobō, 1975.

Izumi Motohide. *Kyōgen de gozaru*. Tokyo: Kōdansha, 1985.

Kanai Kiyomitsu. *Noh no kenkyū*. Tokyo: Ōfūsha, 1979.
_____. *Noh to kyōgen*. Tokyo: Meiji shoin, 1977.

Kawaguchi Hisao, ed. *Wakanrōeishu ryōjinhishō*. Nihon koten bungaku taikei, vol. 73. Tokyo: Iwanami shoten, 1979

Kitagawa Tadahiko and Yasuda Akira. *Kyōgenshū*. Nihon koten bungaku zenshū, vol. 35, Tokyo: Shōgakkan, 1972.
_____. "Zeami to Okashi." *Kokubungaku: kaishaku to kanshō* 537 (February1977):62-63.

Kobatake Motoo. *Kyōgen no bigaku*. Tokyo: Sōgensha, 1986.

Kobayashi Seki. *Kyōgen hyakuban*. Tokyo: Heibonsha, 1980.
_____. *Kyōgen o tanoshimu*. Tokyo: Heibonsha, 1976.
_____. *Kyōgenshi kenkyū*. Tokyo: Wanya, 1974.
_____ et al., eds. *Yōkyoku kyōgenshū*. Tokyo: Meijisha, 1978.
_____. *Noh to kyōgen no sekai*. Tokyo: Kōdansha, 1982.

Konishi Jinichi. *Sōgi*. Tokyo: Chikuma shobō, 1972.

Koyama Hiroshi, ed., *Noh kyōgen: kyōgen no sekai*, vol. 5. Tokyo: Iwanami shoten, 1987.
_____. ed. *Noh kyōgen: kyōgen kanshō annai*, vol. 7. Tokyo: Iwanami shoten, 1990.
_____ ed. *Kyōgenshū*, vols.1, 2. Nihon koten bungaku taikei, vols. 42-43. Tokyo: Iwanami shoten, 1972.
_____ et al., eds. *Yōkyokushū*, vols.1, 2. Nihon koten bungaku zenshū, vols. 33-34. Tokyo: Shōgakkan, 1976.

_____ et al., eds. *Yōkyoku kyōgen.* Nihon koten bungaku, vol. 22. Tokyo: Kadokawa shoten, 1977.

_____. "Kyōgen no kotei." *Bungaku* 16 (July 1948): 408-418.

_____. "Kyōgen no hensen." *Bungaku* 24 (July 1956): 789-832.

_____. "Kotei zen no kyōgen." *Kokugo to kokubungaku* 318, 319 (October and November 1950): 71-77, 19-26.

_____. "Noh to kyōgen."*Kokugo to kokubungaku* 684 (February 1981):1-21.

_____. "Kyōgen no kotoba." *Kokugo to kokubungaku* 312 (April 1950): 38-47.

_____. "Kyōgen to noh: 'ai no mono' to shite no kanten kara." *Hikakubungaku kenkyū* 35 (August 1979): 1-19.

_____. "Kyōgen no warai." *Gengo seikatsu* 59 (August 1956): 33-40.

Kyōgen zenshū. Tokyo: Kokuminbunko kankōkai, 1914.

Masuda Shōzō. *Noh no dezain.* Tokyo: Heibonsha, 1976.

Matsuda Tamotsu. *Noh kyōgen nyūmon.* Tokyo: Bunken shuppan, 1976.

Matsumoto Kamematsu. *Kyōgen rikugi no kenkyū.* Tokyo: Wanya, 1972.

Matsumoto Shinpachirō. "Kyōgen ni okeru toshi to nōson." *Bungaku* 16 (December 1948): 723-732.

Miyake Tokurō. *Komai utai.* Tokyo: Wanya, 1974.

_____. *Kyōgen no midokoro.* Tokyo: Wanya, 1974.

Murayama Shūichi. *Yamabushi no rekishi.* Tokyo: Hanawa shobō, 1979.

Nakayama Hiroaki, ed. *Kyōgenki.* Nihon bungaku taikei, vol. 22. Tokyo: Kabundō, 1931.

Nihon bungaku kenkyū shiryō kankōkai. *Yōkyoku kyōgen.* Tokyo: Yūseidō, 1981.

Nishio Minoru, Tanaka Makoto, Kanai Kiyomitsu and Ikeda Hiroshi. *Yōkyoku kyōgen.* Kokugo kokubungakushi taisei, vol. 8. Tokyo: Sanseidō, 1977.

Nogami Toyoichirō, ed. *Yōkyoku zenshū.* Tokyo: Chūō kōron, 1971.
_____. ed. *Nōgaku zensho,* vol. 5. Tokyo: Sōgensha, 1980.
_____. "Kyōgen no fūshi to kaigyaku." *Bungaku* 15 (August 1947): 497-507.

Nomura Mansaku. *Tarō Kaja o ikiru.* Tokyo: Hakusuisha, 1984.

Nomura Manzō. *Kyōgen geiwa.* Tokyo: Wanya, 1981.
_____. *Kyōgen men.* Tokyo: Wanya, 1956.
_____. *Kyōgen no michi.* Tokyo: Wanya, 1967.

Nonomura Kaizō and Andō Tsunejirō, eds. *Kyōgen shūsei.* Tokyo: Nōgaku shorin, 1974.
_____. ed. *Kyōgen sanbyakubanshū.* Tokyo: Toyamabō, 1938.

Nose Asaji. *Noh kyōgen jōruri kabuki.* Tokyo: Ibundō, 1951.
_____. *Nōgaku genryū kō.* Tokyo: Iwanami shoten, 1972.

Omote Akira. *Nōgakushi shinkō.* Vol.1. Tokyo: Wanya, 1979.

Sasano Ken. *Noh kyōgen: Ōkura Torahiro bon.* Vols. 1-3. Tokyo: Iwanami shoten, 1977-78.

Satake Akihiro. *Gekokujō no bungaku.* Tokyo: Chikuma shobō, 1982.

Shigeyama Sengorō. *Sengorō kyōgen banashi.* Tokyo: Kōdansha, 1983.

Shigeyama Sennojō. "Kyōgen no enshutsu," in Araki Yoshio, *Nihon bungaku shinchō.* Osaka: Sōgensha, 1957.
_____. *Kyōgen yakusha hinekure handaiki.* Tokyo: Iwanami shoten,1987.

Shigeyama Sensaku. *Kyōgen hachijūnen.* Kyoto: Miyako shuppan, 1951.

Suzuki Tōzō, ed. *Seisuishō: sengoku no warai banashi,* Tōyō bunko, vol. 31. Tokyo: Heibonsha, 1981.

Taguchi Kazuo. *Kyōgen ronkō.* Tokyo: Miyai shoten, 1977.

Takano Tatsuyuki. *Men to kyōgen.* Tokyo: Tokyodō, 1942.

Tanaka Yutaka. *Zeami geijutsu ronshū.* Tokyo: Shinchōsha, 1976.

Tanizaki Junichirō. *Tsuki to kyōgenshi.* Tokyo: Chūōkōron, 1981.

Toida Michizō. *Kyōgen: rakuhaku shita kamigami no henbō.* Tokyo: Heibonsha, 1973.
_____. *Noh geiron.* Tokyo: Tokyodō, 1942.

Tsuruta Kyūsaku. *Kyōgen zenshū. (Kyōgenki).* Tokyo: Kokumin bunkokaikan, 1914.

Wakamori Tarō. *Wakamori Tarō chosakushū.* Tokyo: Kōbundō, 1980.

Yamamoto Tōjirō. *Kyōgen no susume.* Tokyo: Tamagawa daigaku shuppan, 1978.

Yokomichi Mario. *Nohgeki no kenkyū.* Tokyo: Iwanami shoten, 1986.
_____ et al., eds. *Noh to kyōgen no sekai.* Tokyo: Heibonsha, 1980.
_____ ed. *Yōkyokushū.* Vols.1, 2. Nihon koten bungaku taikei, vols. 40, 41. Tokyo: Iwanami shoten, 1980.

Yonekura Toshiaki. *Waranbegusa kenkyū.* Tokyo: Kazama shobō, 1973.

Yoshida Kōichi, ed. *Izumiryū kyōgenshū Kumogata bon.* 20 vols. Tokyo: Kotenbunkobon, 1955.

CORNELL EAST ASIA SERIES

For ordering information, please contact:

> Cornell East Asia Series
> East Asia Program
> Cornell University
> 140 Uris Hall
> Ithaca, NY 14853-7601
> USA
> (607) 255-6222.